Anthems of Hope

Ben Courson

Dedicated to my wife Necia:
whom I love and adore with all my heart

Acknowledgements

First and foremost, Emily Fleischer who painstakingly and tirelessly edited each page and every chapter of both *Anthems* and my previous work, *Anthology*. To you I owe a debt which only Heaven can reward adequately. Thank you.

Also my sister Mary for her invaluable encouragement; Kat Walker for her amazing cover artwork; Dave Cooper for being my Aaron and Hur; and Searchlight for believing in this project.

Lastly and most importantly, my wife Necia who walked with me through each and every stage of the writing process. Her insights and contributions were vital. You are the best.

Contents

Preface   11

The Adventure of Hope   13

A Giant for a Shepherd   17

Bravely Authentic   23

Faith in a Furnace   27

The War for Souls   37

No Matter the Odds   41

Moving Mountains   49

Soaring Sea   55

Worry's Dark Mirage   67

Walking in the Miraculous   73

Overcoming Twilight   79

Resurrected Belief   83

Divided Hearts Will Break   89

Perceiving the Unseen   93

Fighting for Harmony   101

Captive Liberty   105

Unlocking the Fervor of Praise   111

Leprous Conceit   115

The Heart's Mirror   121

Amongst My Heroes   125

Beaming Hope to the Nations   131

Whirlwind Legacy   135

Determine Eternity   145

A Prisoner's Destiny   149

Race to the Future   155

Preface

Everyone needs hope.

It's hope that enables us to live rather than merely exist. Our Creator is the God of hope, and He has destined us to be creatures of purpose. He did not create us to get through the days . . . He created us to conquer.

The aim of this book is to inspire us to discover hope in every aspect of our walk with God. Each chapter is a call to abandon the wilderness of unbelief and take on the giants of the promised land. Many of the chapters are retold Bible stories, giving us a chance to instill our own imagination into the story. Of course, we cannot know all the details of the classic tales of old, but they *really did happen*. That blows my mind. These characters were human just like us, but they had faith in a God who was bigger than they were, and they witnessed the removal of mountains.

Other chapters are windows into the truths of Scripture: winning souls to Christ, worshipping with our whole hearts, storing treasure in Heaven, praying like giants of faith, etc. These windows may not have the clarity of experience and wisdom, but rather the tint of youth to aid us in seeing the truth with eyes like a child. I know for me, my vision can be easily blinded by doubt, and I have held words of simple encouragement so close, and that is what I hope to do for others in this collection of writings: awaken the sixth sense of faith, and put to bed the tendency to walk by sight.

May this book send your soul on a journey toward God so that you might sail the once-charted waters of child-like faith and explore the hidden kingdom of miracles and dreams.

Lord, I pray that Your Spirit would go before each page so that we can discover the fingerprints You leave behind. Sing these anthems of hope into our souls. You use the foolish things to confound the wise, so I pray that You would use this book to impact lives. Kindle a fire of passion in our hearts for You, and make it to shine as a bright light that defeats the darkness. In Jesus name, amen.

One

The Adventure of Hope

Are you sad and empty? Do you feel like you're barely getting by? Is your hope a fading sunset, slowly falling behind the mountains you can't seem to scale?

There is one place where the sun always shines, where there is no darkness or shadow of turning. There is a place where your mountains can be moved and your faith can stand firm. A refuge you can run to where hope is strong and unashamed.

The presence of God.

In God's presence, your emptiness will be consumed by fullness of joy, and your sorrows will be lost in newfound pleasures. You will discover a life that's abundant and a light that ignites fire in your soul. In Him you will gain stars to grace your darkest galaxies, and bold promises to pierce the most foreboding clouds.

The closer you get to Him, the closer He will get to you, and the closer He gets to you the closer you are to Heaven on earth. The King has humbled

Himself to give His kingdom to our broken worlds, and belief to repair our broken hearts. He can vitalize your fading hope and resurrect your dying passion.

The Bible says that after Jesus died, several of His friends went to visit His tomb, but upon their arrival they discovered the tomb was empty. They didn't find Jesus in the cemetery, because He was not among the dead. He was among the living. They would never find Him in places of death, and neither will we. We cannot find the Lord if we approach His presence like we would approach a tomb. If we come to Him expecting a lifeless, boring, and unexciting experience then we're not going to find Him. If our walk with God feels dead it is because we're looking in all the wrong places.

The Gospel means "good news." Why do we treat it as if it were bad news? Why do we crawl under the weight of the "Gospel," laboriously struggling to carry it to the world? The Bible says "how beautiful on the mountains are the feet of those who bring good news and salvation." The Gospel is not a burden to carry but wings to inspire our flight.

Jesus is alive. The holes in His hands can close the hole inside of your heart, and the scar on His side promises He will always be by your side.

Touch His wounds, and your scars will heal.

Jesus did not come to burden us, but to take away our burdens and convey His rest to us. He came to devastate our darkness and shine His peace into our souls. The Bible says He is the light of the world. He is not called the rain of the world or the dictating gray cloud of the world, but the brilliant, dazzling, dancing light that brings hope to our worlds. He will lead you through the valley of shadows and death into the light of life. The road is arduous, but the end will defend your journey.

You're closing in on your destiny, so fight hard and stand despite the fallen soldiers all around you. Don't be afraid of the dangers you encounter on the way. God is writing your story. Without danger there is no adventure, and life without adventure is not life at all.

There is nothing more adventurous, fulfilling, or exhilarating than traveling through life with God. He is the author of our faith, and He writes the stories that mean the most to us. He created the miraculous world where a fisherman walks on water, where a prophet calls fire from Heaven, where a man spends days in the belly of a fish, where a child slays a giant, where a leader divides the ocean, and where a God dies for His creation.

That doesn't sound very boring to me.

And the adventure has only begun. The story continues with you. Jesus will be the way you walk, the truth you believe, and the life that you live. He will be with you, even to the ending of the world.

A new hope dawns on the horizon of your dreams.

Two

A Giant for a Shepherd

My rapid thoughts raced the swift beating of my heart. Logic collided with the insanity of my faith. I had never been more nervous in my life.

What was I getting myself into?

A cool breeze shuffled my shaggy red hair. A few milky clouds peacefully strolled overhead. A small bird chirped sunnily beside me, leaking a little serenity into my disquieted soul. I carefully weighed my options. So many weapons to choose from, and I had to pick just the right ones. Only, today my weapons were not to be chosen from an arsenal . . . but from a brook.

The freedom of my beloved country was on the line. Goliath, a ferocious giant of the Philistine army, challenged my people to send forth a warrior to fight him in a contest of champions. If our representative could defeat him, then the Philistines would be our slaves. But if Goliath won, we would be their slaves. Day after day he strutted in front of the Israelite army with his arrogant taunts, intimidating even the bravest men. No one dared to challenge him.

That's when I stepped in: the shepherd boy from Bethlehem. I proposed to fight the proud Philistine who defied the name of my God. People said that he was the greatest soldier on the earth, but what was this giant in the eyes of my LORD? Goliath was a mere ant under the omnipotent heel of the God of Israel. With God on my side, nothing could stop me, no matter how young or small I might be.

But as I gazed into the brook, reality slowly crept up on me. What if I was wrong? Could this be the biggest mistake of my life? If God was not in this, then surely my doom was at hand. Maybe I was knocking on death's door with some false sense of nobility, foolishly inviting national slavery and personal destruction with my arms wide open. Maybe my youthful zeal had clouded any wisdom that I previously possessed.

Perhaps this was the end.

But wait . . . I've had this feeling before. This is the feeling I always get just before something great is about to happen. This same cold sensation has come over my heart before. Yes . . . yes, I remember now! I remember the time my sheep were threatened by that lion with the fierce teeth. When I saw him approaching my flock, sudden doubt and fear clouded my mind then too. Yet deep within my soul I felt the hand of God reach into me, planting a little seed of courage. That was all I needed. I raised my eyes, ran with all the speed I could muster, and tackled the lion. It was as if some strange, impulsive power came upon me from above, and I seized the lion by his hair and beat him with my club until his dead carcass lay motionless in the open field.

I killed the beast that threatened my sheep then, and I would kill the giant that threatened God's sheep now. Today I would be a shepherd for Israel. Today I would kill this foul giant in the strength of the LORD.

As the seed of courage began to blossom in my soul, I reached into the brook and collected my final stone. I whirled around to set out for the battlefield and was surprised to find thousands of Israelite soldiers watching me with wide eyes. They silently parted, creating a small pathway between them. I marched through with eyes steadfast ahead, and a sudden shout came from one of the soldiers. "For the God of Israel!" he cried. Fists were immediately thrown to the sky, and all together the soldiers roared, "For the God of Israel!"

Hot tears welled in my eyes as I soldiered on through the reassuring crowd. Caught up in the moment, I found no reason to fight back my joyful tears. All the soldiers (many old enough to be my parents, all taller and stronger than me) patted my shoulders with heartening words. I clutched my shepherd's staff resolved and determined, then walked onto the battlefield.

There was Goliath, standing still as stone.

He was a lot bigger than I expected, and I was already expecting him to be gargantuan.

His eyes were fierce with blazing rage. A formidable helmet sat on his oversized head, and a thick coat of scale armor added more intimidation to his already-imposing stature. In one hand he held an iron-gripped spear and with the other a fearsome bronze javelin. A young warrior with a sneer on his face fortified the giant with a protective shield, and the vast Philistine army stood firm behind their celebrated champion.

Goliath swaggered out to meet me with his shield bearer in front of him. His strides were long and his manner was stern. He halted when he was still a good thirty paces from me, carefully looked me up and down . . .

And then burst out laughing.

"Am I a dog," he roared contemptuously, "that you come at me with a stick?" He walked towards me laughing wildly and, when he could catch his breath, he cursed me in the names of his gods. "Come here," he cried, "and I will give your flesh to the birds of the air and the beasts of the field!"

Mockery and bloodlust sparkled in his eyes. His enormous fingers stroked the grip of each of his deadly weapons. He licked his lips and flashed a hideous smile, exposing all of his crooked yellow teeth.

I couldn't believe the words that then came out of my mouth. It was as if God borrowed my voice and did all the talking, using me as nothing more than a channel for Him to speak through. I looked up at Goliath and shouted, "You come against me with sword, spear, and javelin, but I come against you in the name of the LORD of hosts, the God of the armies of Israel, whom you have defied. Today the LORD will conquer you, and I will kill you and cut off your head. And then I will give the dead bodies of your men to the birds of the air and the beasts of the earth, and the whole world will know that there is a God in Israel! And everyone will know that the LORD does not need weapons to rescue his people. The battle is the LORD's, and He will give you into our hands."

Goliath's repulsive smile suddenly disappeared. He gritted his teeth, furrowed his brow, and moved in for the attack. Adrenaline racing, I ran at him faster than I had ever run in my life. I reached into my shepherd's bag with my eyes still locked onto his and pulled out a small stone. I put the stone in my sling, whirled it around, and hurled it at his head. The release felt just right, and time seemed to slow as the small stone sailed through the air.

He had no time to duck.

The stone connected and sank deep into the center of his forehead. Dumbfounded, he reeled back and forth several times. He looked at me for a moment in utter confusion, then fell face down to the ground.

The earth trembled beneath my feet as his massive body came down with a reverberating thud. My heart seemed to pound even louder than his crash. I hurried over to the fallen giant and stood on his back. I pulled his sword from its sheath and brandished it victoriously. The blade glistened in the clear sunlight.

And with one fateful, death-dealing stroke, I chopped off Goliath's head.

Deafening Israelite shouts filled the air. Terrified Philistine soldiers fled in retreat. Impossible joy flooded my soul. God fought the battle.

And He never loses.

Three

Bravely Authentic

Do you ever feel like you're just not quite good enough? Have you gone through the endless cycle of comparing yourself with others and, although you've discovered that it gets you nowhere, you just can't seem to stop? Is your approach to life so different and your mind-set so unique that you sometimes catch yourself thinking that there must be something wrong with you?

Whether it be from the good intentions of those close to us, or the ridiculous propaganda that the world throws at us, we are constantly told who we are supposed to be.

The magazine on the shelf says you have to look like her.

Your textbook tells you the facts "you'd be a fool not to believe!"

A well-meaning friend whispers, "Just fit in and do what everyone else does . . . it's the only way we survive."

But you are not defined by the constant demands hurled at you: you are defined by your response to them. Conforming is easy . . . and incredibly boring. Going against the crowd is terrifying, but it's exciting, heroic, and absolutely satisfying. To miss the adventure would be tragic, and if you wear a mask you'll be just another face in the crowd. You are the only person in the entire world that can be you. The world needs you, not you trying to be someone else.

Change starts when one brave soul dares to defy the status quo.

Be bravely authentic, because the only way to make a difference is to be different. Don't blend in and let your surroundings transform you, be yourself and you will transform your surroundings. Never cave in when you're pressured to be something you're not. How will you change things if you're the one being changed? If you step out in faith, you will probably step on some toes . . . but you will be stronger than your fear of what others think about you when you are performing only for an audience of One.

Be the best version of yourself, because sincerity will make your most beautiful characteristics shine. Learn from others, and find deep within yourself the captivating qualities you see in them, but in the end, don't be anyone other than who God created you to be. The more secure you are in who He's called you to be, the less you will copy, judge, and compare yourself to others. There will always be someone in your life you can compare yourself to, but your comparisons will only create pride, jealousy, and depression until the person you could've been is consumed by the darkness that now defines who you are.

Race not against others, but against the person your potential says you can be.

Reach for the stars and reject second best. God is still in the process of creating you, so put Him first, and He will design your desires and dreams to be a perfect reflection of the plans He already has for your life. Your unique dreams and thoughts may not make sense to others, but they make sense to the Lord. He has entrusted to you special gifts, and you need all of them for your mission here on earth: each one is a tool that can fix broken hearts and repair damaged lives.

You are a heavenly being, and this world is nothing more than a road you must travel to get to your real home. In order to be the best version of yourself here on earth, you must practice now who you're going to be in Heaven. Imitate Christ, and no one else; His authentic example will give you the courage to be yourself. As you follow Him, your insecurity will transform into humble confidence, and your weakness will gradually disappear into His strength. You will gain the keys of your calling when you confess that Jesus is your savior, and your identity will become a rock when you are broken on the Chief Cornerstone. You will catch souls as a fisher of men when you no longer find your security in the career your net can bring, and you will overcome the intimidation of giants when you take off Saul's armor to fight with your sling.

The Lord knew exactly what He was doing when He created you, and He has created a masterpiece. No one can be you as good as you can. Free your burdened soul from conformity.

Have the courage to be yourself.

Four

Faith in a Furnace

The decree was made. The music was about to begin. The golden image loomed ominously above us.

This was the biggest decision of our lives.

Worship the statue and live, or remain loyal to God and die?

Nebuchadnezzar, the king of Babylon, recently erected a ninety-foot high statue. He summoned all the leaders of his domain and demanded that they worship the image. If anyone should disobey the king's command and refuse to bow down, he would pay the penalty of death in the flames of a blazing furnace.

For God, that was a price I was willing to pay.

I looked into the eyes of my friends, Shadrach and Meshach, and discovered that they too had made up their minds.

"I bow only to the LORD," said Shadrach.

"Whether by life or death," Meshach added, "I will serve the God of Israel."

"The fiery furnace it is," I agreed. "Gladly I go to the flames for my LORD."

The orchestra began to play, and the enormous crowd bowed down to the image. In perfect uniformity, their foreheads touched the ground as they paid obeisance to King Nebuchadnezzar and the Empire of Babylon. No one dared to defy the king's edict.

But we didn't move a single muscle.

The gold of the statue shone with the reflection of the afternoon sun. I felt so insignificant beneath this giant image, so exposed in the midst of this sea of blindly obedient subjects. My heart raced. We couldn't get away with our insubordinate stand for long. The furnace was near. I fought with its imaginary flames in my head.

Beautiful notes blended together to fill the sky. The song was dazzling, mesmerizing, as if to cast some strange spell on the crowd. It managed to take hold of the deepest emotions, issuing a generous threat to invade the soul. The rising melodies invited my friends and me to succumb to what everyone else was doing. But no matter how captivating the music may have been, we knew where our allegiances lay. That allegiance could not be broken. No matter the cost, nothing would bend our knee.

The song ended. The beating of my heart slowed. Somehow my knees weren't shaking. My head was held high. I looked over at Shadrach and Meshach, and their eyes mirrored the very confidence I felt in my own soul. God had bestowed on each of us a gift of courage in our time of most dire need. I firmly grabbed each of their shoulders and looked intently into their eyes. I smiled and gave a nod. These might be our last moments, and I couldn't be happier to spend them with my best friends.

Several large men rushed towards us. They snatched each of us by the arm and pulled us through the crowd. I could almost feel the relief of the people as we passed by them: an overwhelming joy that they were not in our position, that they were not to be burned in the furnace.

The guards released us when we finally arrived at the presence of the king. His brow was furrowed and his eyes blazed furiously. We looked at him without so much as blinking. He was clearly astonished to find no hint of fear in our expressions. He opened his mouth to speak, then closed it again on second thought. He tilted his head curiously, and his countenance suddenly altered. A mask of artificial forgiveness fell over his face.

"Is it true, Shadrach, Meshach, and Abednego," he said at last in an exaggeratedly gracious tone, "that you refuse to serve my gods or to worship the gold statue that I have set up? I will give you one more chance. If you bow down and worship the statue I have made when you hear the sound of the musical instruments, all will be well."

The corners of his mouth turned up as he inclined his head. But his countenance turned slightly malevolent when he said his next words. Evil intent crept into his voice.

"But if you refuse," he continued, "you will be thrown immediately into the blazing furnace. What god will be able to rescue you then?"

With our unflinching gazes still fastened on the king, we replied, "O Nebuchadnezzar, we do not need to defend ourselves before you. If we are thrown into the blazing furnace, the God whom we serve is able to save us. He will rescue us from your power, Your Majesty. But even if He doesn't, Your Majesty can be sure that we will never serve your gods or worship the statue that you have set up."

Nebuchadnezzar's features wholly transformed. Throwing off whatever was left of his mask of forgiveness, his forehead scrunched together and his complexion became sizzling red. His lips pursed together as if that alone could keep his face from exploding. Blistering wrath seemed to take on the form of white-hot flames in his eyes. He raised an indignant fist and demanded the furnace be heated seven times hotter than usual. The fire burning in his eyes seemed even fiercer than the one we were about to be thrown into.

Three burly soldiers hastily bound us in ropes. They lifted us effortlessly and carried us to the fire. Still a good ten paces from the furnace, the soldiers began to stagger due to the intense temperatures. For some reason, though, I couldn't feel any heat emitting from the furnace. Apparently Shadrach and Meshach were unaffected by the heat as well, because when I glanced over at them I saw the same puzzled look on their faces that must've been on mine.

Streams of sweat raced down the soldiers' skin. Each one lifted his hand to shield his body from the fatal temperatures, and turned back to the king. They shook their heads helplessly to signal that they couldn't take another step.

"Cast them in the fire!" Nebuchadnezzar screeched. "Or I'll throw you in with them!"

The well-disciplined soldiers inched toward the mouth of the furnace until they were just close enough to throw us in. With a mighty heave they pitched us into the inferno. As we flew through the air, white flames leapt from the fire and struck the soldiers down, killing them instantly. They had met their doom . . . but we were still alive! No . . . not just alive, but completely unharmed! The ropes binding us caught fire and disintegrated in a matter of seconds. I rose to my feet and looked inquisitively at the wild blazes splashing around me. The flames were taller than I was, and they swirled furiously around my body until I was covered in a garment of fire. But I wasn't burned. I wasn't even sweating!

Shadrach, Meshach, and I glanced at one another wide-eyed and speechless.

Could this really be happening?

We looked at the flames, then at each other, then at the flames again. Comprehension dawned: this really *was* happening! This was an actual *miracle.* We raised clenched fists and shouted triumphantly. We marched around the furnace and through the flames, cheering and laughing. We made certain to take in every moment of this once-in-a-lifetime adventure.

All of a sudden, I glimpsed a glowing figure through the blazes. He walked slowly towards us, and I immediately recognized Him as none other than an Angel of God! His countenance glimmered like distant lightning, and His garments were whiter than freshly fallen snow. His wavy hair was like wool, and His eyes were as fiery daggers that pierced my soul the very moment I gazed into their depths. His feet were reflective bronze, as if refined in this very furnace. He was powerfully built and unnaturally tall, and His fierce majesty would have frightened even the most valiant of men. If God Himself ever had a Son, then this had to be Him.

He didn't say a word but simply walked around and gazed at us. His eyes spoke more than any utterance could. *I have been sent by God,* they seemed to say, *to shield you from the flames. Your knees bow before the Living God alone. Well done, O mighty men of God . . . well done.*

The message in His keen eyes penetrated my being. I was so intent upon this captivating Angel that I'm uncertain how long we were in the furnace, but when I heard a voice from outside I whirled around to see King Nebuchadnezzar about fifteen paces away, shouting to be heard over the roaring fire.

"Shadrach, Meshach, and Abednego," he called, "servants of the Most High God, come out! Come here!"

I turned to face the Angel once more, but He had vanished. My friends and I exchanged dumb-founded expressions, shaking our heads in utter amazement at the brief appearance of this Heavenly Visitor. It felt as if the presence of God had eternally marked the furnace, and there was no place else I'd rather be. None of us desired to leave. But we knew we couldn't stay in here forever.

"It's time," said Shadrach. "Now we go back into the world as living miracles."

Meshach and I nodded our agreement. It was time. We stepped out of the fire with smiles beaming from our faces. Throngs of people quickly formed around us. I noticed that these were the same people who had just bowed down to the golden image. Disbelieving gasps accompanied their inspection of us. Not a hair on our heads was singed, not a single thread of our clothes was scorched, and we didn't even carry the scent of smoke.

Nebuchadnezzar ordered the crowd to make room. He rapidly circled around us wringing his hands in bewilderment, then touched us to examine our skin and clothes for burn marks . . . or he may have just been trying to figure out if we were even real. After several moments of silent awe, he finally realized that this was, indeed, nothing short of a miracle. He lifted his hands and shouted, "Praise to the God of Shadrach, Meshach, and Abednego! He sent His Angel to rescue His servants who trusted in Him. They defied the king's command and were willing to die rather than serve or worship any god except their own God. Therefore, I make this decree: if any people, whatever their race or nation or language, speak a word against the God of Shadrach, Meshach, and Abednego, they will be torn limb from limb, and their houses will be crushed into heaps of rubble. There is no other god who can rescue like this!"

I could hardly believe my ears: the same king who attempted to execute us for our loyalty to God only a few moments ago was now giving God praise. Now the LORD was to be honored throughout all the earth, and it all began with a simple stand of faith. The ardent flames of devotion have proved even more powerful than the fires of persecution. When God is on our side, and when we choose to be on His, the world can change.

We have nothing to fear.

Five

The War for Souls

The world is full of souls searching for meaning and purpose in life. Longing for a place they can call home, they wander on the broad path day and night but are unable to find what they're looking for. Flames of darkness seek to claim their destiny. Death hunts their thoughts, leaving their minds in the grave even before they die. Satan dangles hollow pleasures as bait for their hungry eyes, teasing their desires with a promise of fulfillment that seems so close but is always one impossible step away.

Blindly they follow the piper to their doom.

We can catch them before they reach the land of darkness and flames. We can cast the net of the Gospel into the darkest waters and fish for men submerged in the world. We can lead them to salvation's marvelous light.

We can rescue them from their tragic end.

The power of salvation is in our hands. It's up to us to give it out. The Lord has entrusted us with the work of building His Kingdom on the earth, and each one of us has been given the urgent mission to evangelize. The harvest is plentiful and souls are seeking out the truth, but our time is running out. We have been given only a short while to finish our task. There are so many people who are searching for a savior, and they crave the fruit that springs from the lives of others. But how will they grow fruit unless someone plants God's Word in the soil of their hearts?

Will you labor for the harvest of this generation?

The Bible promises that if we convert many to righteousness, we will shine like stars forever in Heaven. There is no limit to the souls we can win to Christ if we will imitate how He lived and valiantly continue the message He preached. If we will unite under the banner of the Gospel, we can pull the Kingdom of God down to our world. Our combined lights will put to flight the darkness that has enslaved souls for far too long.

The torch of the Gospel is in our hands. The course is before us. The race has begun . . .

Run the Gospel to the corners of the earth and save as many people as you can before you die. Storm the gates of hell and do battle with the Father of Lies. Free souls held captive in the prisons of delusion. Turn the key of truth that will set them free. Unleash the sword of the Spirit on the watchful demons who seek to reclaim the prisoners you rescue. Link shields with your fellow warriors, and your fellowship of faith will create an indestructible defense to quench every fiery dart. Do not be slowed by the twisted lies the enemy whispers into your ear, but put on the belt of truth so you can finish your course without falling. Cover your mind with the helmet of salvation and fill your thoughts with Heaven. Run as fast as you can to deliver souls from the kingdom of darkness: the shoes of the Gospel will give you the speed required to obtain the heavenly crown. Guard your heart from the evil that would destroy your witness. Protect it with the breastplate of righteousness. Follow the Captain of your Salvation into the darkness so you can plant the glowing seeds of God's Word. Do not fear, because you will reap a harvest of light if you do not faint.

Endure hardships as a good soldier of Jesus Christ. Follow Him to the death. Stand your ground and find common ground. Let your voice be heard; make it echo in eternity. Etch names in the Lamb's Book of Life as a pen in the hands of the Author of Faith. Shine your light and emit the joy of the Lord so that others will chase after what you have. Your smile can inspire a world of hope in someone's heart. Never relinquish the cross you carry on the road from this world to the next. Bear it gallantly beside your brothers and sisters, and your courageous example will awaken the greatness in others so that they pick up their own cross and follow you on your journey. Heroically run into the flames and pull people out. Never forget that saving them is more important than saving your reputation. Put on the armor of light, and fight the good fight.

The war for souls is waged.

Six

No Matter the Odds

The contest was about to begin. This was the supreme test—the test of the gods.

Baal vs. the God of Israel.

Ahab, the wicked king of Israel, stood with his arms folded, an expression of contempt smeared across his face. At his side was the vile Queen Jezebel. A murderous fire smoldered in her eyes as she glared at me. Behind them hundreds of pagan prophets waited anxiously for the competition to commence. All around were swarms of Israelite spectators. And I, Elijah, was the LORD's lone representative.

"How much longer will you waver," I asked my countrymen, "hobbling between two opinions? If the LORD is God, follow Him! But if Baal is God, then follow him!"

Complete silence. Nobody had the audacity to speak up. Guilty consciences were revealed on hundreds of faces. The people were unable to make up their minds as to which god was to be served. Their loyalty was divided. They were in the wrong, and they knew it. They knew they couldn't live like this forever.

I stared at their faces, one by one, hoping that my gaze could somehow pierce their souls with truth. I couldn't wait for the match to begin because I knew, beyond a shadow of a doubt, that my God would win. Even though it appeared I was the only one who refused to bow the knee to Baal, I knew who the real God was. And if I was the only one left to stand for Him, then I would gladly stand alone.

The rules of the contest were simple. Two bulls were required: one for me and one for the four hundred and fifty prophets of Baal. They would pick the bull of their choice, cut it into pieces, lay it on the wood of their altar, and call on their god. Then I would prepare my altar, chop up the other bull, and pray to the LORD. The god who answered by setting fire to the wood under the sacrifice would prove to be the true God.

The odds were in their favor. They had four hundred and fifty on their side. I was by myself. They were given the privilege of going first, selecting the bull of their liking, and taking as much time as they needed to pray to their god. Even the very mountain we stood on was considered to be the sacred dwelling place of Baal.

But I knew that odds meant nothing to God.

The prophets of Baal built the altar, prepared their sacrifice, then gathered in close together and bowed their heads. They began murmuring petitions to Baal. Their whispers seemed to transform the atmosphere. When we first congregated, there was a feeling of excitement in the air. Now it felt a dark, satanic presence blanketed the mountaintop. I could sense an invisible warfare all around us, as if swords of angels and demons clashed in our very midst! The angels were obviously winning because the prophets were unable to summon fire from their god.

A hint of desperation could be heard in their voices when no answer came. They raised their hands in the air and began to pray louder. But still no fire came. They then huddled together, rested their arms on each other's shoulders, swayed back and forth, and chanted darkly. Their low, ominous voices were in unison. The ritual was so disturbing that I could feel goosebumps forming on my arms.

But Baal was eerily silent.

Still, they weren't ready to give up. They broke their huddle and started to dance freakishly around the altar. Their arms flailed about as they hopped around. Some were singing as they twirled and skipped while others hummed with their eyes closed as if to conjure up the spirit of their god. Their prayers turned to spasmodic screams. "O Baal, answer us!" they called.

No reply.

"You'll have to shout louder, for surely he is a god!" I scoffed. "Perhaps he is daydreaming, or is engaged in business. Or maybe he is away on a trip, or is asleep and needs to be wakened."

Infuriated by my mockery, they shouted even louder to Baal. Beads of sweat rolled off their bodies as they danced even more frantically in their futile attempt to gain the attention of their god. They leapt onto the altar and leapt off again, screeching at the top of their lungs, and at this point I wondered if I was going to lose my hearing. Their eyes were wide and wild, waiting expectantly for the wood to ignite.

But there was no answer.

Then, following their bizarre custom, they slashed their skin with knives and spears. Crimson blood gushed from their self-inflicted wounds as they cried out impotently. They were madmen howling at their false god, hoping that their blood might move Baal's hand to action.

Their desperation was now turning to blazing

anger, and it seemed they weren't shouting *to* Baal any longer but *at* him. After hours of praying and dancing and lacerating, they finally gave up. Some of them kicked the altar in frustration as they moved aside to join the spectators.

Now it was my turn.

I called all the people to come near the altar of the LORD which was lying in ruins. I selected twelve stones to represent each tribe of Israel, and with them I built the altar. I dug a trench around it, prepared the wood and the sacrifice, and ordered the people to fill four large jars with water and pour it on the bull and the wood. Suspense hung in the air as the great crowd watched me. Three times they poured out the jars of water so that altar, wood, and sacrifice were completely drenched, overflowing the trench that surrounded it. I wanted to show just how powerful the LORD truly was: He could consume the sacrifice with fire even when it was soaked in water.

I stepped forward, lifted my eyes to Heaven, and prayed, "O LORD, God of Abraham, Isaac, and Jacob, prove today that You are God in Israel and that I am Your servant. Prove that I have done all this at Your command. O LORD, answer me! Answer me so these people will know that You have brought them back to Yourself."

Immediately after I said the word *Yourself*, a flood of white fire flashed miles above us, then fell from the sky. It's sizzle shrieked from Heaven so loudly that it seemed the whole world could hear. We shielded our eyes from it's near-blinding light as the piercing flames reached the altar. The fire devoured the bull, burnt the wood and altar to a crisp, consumed the soil, and swooped down to lick up the water from the trench. I felt droplets of perspiration form on my head because of its harsh heat. Its flames danced momentarily before me, destroying any scrap of evidence that an altar had been there. Then it roared back up to Heaven as if God held the flames on a string, sending it down and pulling it up with lightning speed. The miraculous blaze vanished as quickly as it came.

Silence.

Every mouth fell open. Every breath was held. No one moved or even blinked.

The stillness was shattered when one elderly man fell down to the ground and lay prostrate before the living God. Everyone followed his example and fell down on their faces, crying out, "The LORD is God! The LORD is God!"

It was the most beautiful sound I had ever heard, the sound of thousands of Israelite voices declaring the truth. I looked upon the sea of humbled souls, looked up to Heaven to the very spot where the fire had fallen, and was overwhelmed by the power of my God. The God who hears the prayers of His people . . . the God who answers.

Seven

Moving Mountains

Why is it that when we pray, we try to conjure a mountain of faith just to move a mustard seed, when Jesus required only a mustard seed of faith to move a mountain? Why do we complicate prayer and make it so much more difficult than it really is? You can pray this very minute. Right now. You can offer a one-sentence petition, express thanks for a blessing you're now enjoying, or set down this book and go for a five minute walk with the Lord.

Prayer always produces results. It transfers us to Heaven and pulls down God's greatest powers. It reforms our hearts and improves our lives. It is a therapeutic outlet for our deepest emotions and an unimpeded conduit for every perfect gift. It enables a peace that transcends and inspires our purest passions.

When we pray, we must remember we are God's children, and He *wants* to bless us. If our earthly parents love to give us good gifts when we ask them, how much more does our Heavenly

Father love to give good gifts to His children when they pray! He longs to perform mind-blowing works for us, but we miss multitudes of potential blessings simply because we fail to ask. Our slothfulness eradicates the miracles we were meant to walk in and the greatness we could have obtained. We so quickly succumb to the insidious temptations to disbelieve so that the passage connecting our world to Heaven is completely obstructed. There are so many blessings God can't wait to give to us, if we will only ask!

It is truly staggering to know we can access God's throne any time we desire. The God who created the stars and planets, who knows all about you and has power over everything, is literally sitting right next to you this very moment! He waits for you to make use of His presence. He is ready to listen to you and eager to work on your behalf. He *loves* conversing with you. Jesus said, "I no longer call you servants, but friends." Talk to the Lord like you would to your very best friend. Dare to be yourself with God. Say what you mean. There is no sense in hiding who you are from God, seeing that He is the One who created you the way you are and knows you better than you even know yourself. Sometimes it's good to unfold your hands, open your eyes, abandon eloquence, and just go for a walk with Him. You can be more yourself around God than you can around anyone else. The Lord invites you to boldly approach His throne. He gladly asks, "What do you want Me to do for you?"

But if prayer is so remarkable, and if it really does work, then why don't we do it more? The reason is simple: there is a real devil, followed by real demons, who really don't want us to pray. And why should they? Nothing does more to foil their sinister plotting than prayer. So they battle against us. The devil understands prayer advances God's Kingdom and cripples his own, so he evokes all his cunning and subtlety to divert our focus from God's presence. He rides out with his fiendish army to wage war against our minds, striving relentlessly to distract our thoughts and discourage our faith. He whispers lies into our ears until subtle seeds of doubt scatter our prayers. He persuades us that we don't have enough faith to really make any sort of difference, and assures us that we're not quite good enough to approach God's throne. He reminds us that we don't need to pray right now, we can just pray later on, surely we will get around to it eventually!

When your adversary roars these distractions and discouragements into your mind, roar back in prayer. The devil will have no foothold when you acknowledge the reality of this spiritual battle and refuse to lose. Use God's promises as firm foundations for your prayers, because your faith can ward off any attack and thwart even the most treacherous stratagems. Fight for prayer. Fight until the victory is secure.

Don't give up in your prayers because you can't feel God or see Him at work. Sometimes our prayers seem to go unanswered for a long time, our requests feel impossible, and our defiant circumstances challenge prayer's power. But how could we possibly exercise faith if not for this? The Bible says that it is impossible to please God without faith. We live by believing, not by seeing. If there were never times when our requests seem like they'll never come to pass, then our faith would never grow. So do not be afraid to pray for massive things, because He is able to accomplish infinitely more than we would ever dare to ask or hope for. The Lord doesn't want to just give the crippled man a coin or two, He wants to heal his legs. He doesn't only want to lead His people to the Promised Land, but also part the Red Sea on the journey there. He doesn't merely calm the life-threatening storm, but decides to walk on its waves while He's at it. So do not pray as if there were a limit to God's blessings.

His love knows no boundaries, so neither should our prayers. Think of the biggest prayer you can pray, then pray bigger.

Change is just a prayer away.

Don't wait any longer. Get back up and throw your mountains into the sea. Leave your inhibitions behind and recover your passion. No prayer is too big for the Lord, and no prayer is too small for Him either. Nothing is too hard for God. Ask and you will receive, seek and you will find, knock and the door will be opened. The Lord is waiting.

All things are possible if a person believes.

Eight

Soaring Sea

"Why did you bring us out here to die in the wilderness?" screamed a panic-stricken man as he pulled his hair with both hands. "Weren't there enough graves for us in Egypt? Why did you make us leave?"

A weeping woman holding a child in her arms echoed his protest, "Didn't we tell you to leave us alone while we were still in Egypt?"

A burly man wagged his fist and shook his head as he shouted angrily, "Our Egyptian slavery was far better than dying out here in the wilderness."

Millions of enraged Israelite faces scowled at me. Their thunderous complaints seemed to shake the ground beneath my feet. We were caught in a trap.

And I was the one who led them into it.

Our imminent doom marched towards us in the form of Egyptian soldiers. Hundreds of brawny horses hauled spectacular chariots. Pharaoh rode ahead of them, hungry to recapture his prized

slaves. A range of mountains loomed like impen-
etrable prison walls to the right and to the left. The
Red Sea lingered before us, preventing any chance
of escape. The pillar of cloud (which had been sent
to guide us) was parked over the seashore, like an
old gnarled stone in the sky, as if it too had no idea
where to go next.

I looked into the faces of my people, into
the mad terror that sprang from their eyes, and
raised my hands in the air, gesturing for silence. A
hush fell upon the crowd.

"Do not be afraid," I said. "Stand still, and
see the salvation of the LORD, which He will accomplish for you today. The Egyptians that you see
today will never be seen again. The LORD Himself
will fight for you, and you shall hold your peace."

For a moment it seemed the crowd was
placated, but the swift silence was broken when
distant Egyptian battle cries reached our ears. Their
shouts were edged with malice, and new waves of
hysteria crashed upon the vast sea of Israelite faces.
Mothers tried to comfort their screaming children.
Men bellowed their renewed rage. The older women
stood dumbfounded, trembling in terror.

There was only one thing left for me to do.

I cried out to the LORD.

In the midst of the chaos, I found peace as I

immersed my soul in His presence. But while still in the middle of my prayer, I was interrupted by a gentle voice whispering into my ear from behind me. I instinctively opened my eyes and whirled around to see who was speaking to me, but I was not surprised when I didn't find anyone there. I already knew who the voice belonged to. I couldn't help but think back to the first time I heard this voice through the flames of the bush out in the wilderness.

"Why are you crying out to Me?" the LORD said. "Tell the people to get moving! Raise your staff and stretch out your hand over the sea and divide it. Then all the people of Israel will walk through on dry ground. Yet I will harden the hearts of the Egyptians so that they will go in after them. And I will gain glory through Pharaoh and all his army, through his chariots and his horsemen. When I am finished with Pharaoh and his army, all Egypt will know that I am the LORD!"

Suddenly the pillar of cloud stirred and rumbled as if it awakened from a deep sleep. It floated downwards until it was suspended only several feet off the ground, then slowly rolled around our camp. Everyone stopped and watched the miraculous cloud amble to the back of the crowd. When it finally arrived, it pulsated and blackened, creating an impregnable shield between us and the Egyptian army.

With the pillar of cloud protecting us, disabling any potential military advance from behind, I gripped my staff and faced the Red Sea. I took a moment to catch my breath and gather my thoughts. I observed the ocean before me. The water looked so peaceful, undisturbed, untouched by all the turmoil of the day. Small waves glided towards the shore, reflecting the luminous moon above. The distant horizon swallowed the final pink traces of the sun as thousands of stars ignited the darkening sky. As I lifted my eyes to gaze at the faraway galaxies, I was reminded of the promise God gave to our father Abraham—the promise that one day his descendants would be as numerous as the stars. And there we, Abraham's offspring, stood together in numbers matching the stars overhead.

God was faithful to Abraham.

And tonight He would be faithful to Abraham's children.

But my thoughts were disrupted when, all of a sudden, the ocean lit up before my eyes. The watery surface was covered instantly by an incandescence of orange. I turned around to find the source of the light, and my eyes were dazzled by the giant pillar of fire that shone brilliantly behind us. It roared and splashed flames into the night-time sky. This was nothing new; each night the pillar of cloud would transform into a pillar of fire to guide us through the hours of darkness. But still, it never ceased to rob me of my breath. How does God think up something like a pillar of cloud by day that turns into a pillar of fire by night? Incredible.

I marveled at this awe-inspiring fire . . . but I couldn't wait to see what He was about to do with water.

A smile crept onto my face.

I spun toward the sea and raised my staff in the air like a motivated soldier brandishing his sword before charging the front lines. An abrupt silence filled the air. All was still. Time slowed down. The water itself appeared to have turned to stone. This was the breath before the storm because, mere seconds later, an eastern gale rushed upon the sea and howled in our ears. It seemed like God Himself inhaled and blew into the world. I had never seen such a fierce wind in my life. It cut through the water, generating dozens of chaotic waves. Then, all at once, two enormous liquid walls burst into the sky, creating a pathway between them. The transparent surfaces stood straight up and down, soaring high above us. It looked as though they were tall enough to scrape the white stars that sparkled above them. Despite all of the miracles I had seen before this, I couldn't help but wonder if I was dreaming.

If I was, I didn't want to wake up.

Everyone watched in silence (save the inevitable gasps that echoed throughout the camp) stunned by the parted sea. After about ten seconds of open-mouthed staring, the whole camp erupted in cheers and victorious laughter. I found it nearly impossible to contain the joy as I stood with my people and reveled in this monumental moment. But when I looked at the towering vertical waters to my right and left, I have to admit that it was fairly daunting to step between them. I mean, if they were to collapse I would be instantly crushed.

I breathed deeply, then took one step. Then another. Then several more. I glanced up at the roaring walls and, sure enough, they didn't collapse! I walked on, laughing and marveling as I traveled through the Red Sea. After I had taken my first few steps, I heard millions of feet shuffling behind me. Together we journeyed to the other side.

The pillar of fire followed closely behind us, illuminating the dry path before our feet. A cool, gentle mist floated down from the ocean barriers. On either side of us, dozens of colorful animals

swam by. Three vividly orange Clownfish grace-
fully maneuvered through the water at eye-level.
A majestic Polyclad Flatworm flaunted its beautiful tones. An octopus sprawled out its limbs high
above us, lazily wandering by. Blending in cleverly
with its surroundings, a cuttlefish concealed itself
as a nearby Giant Moray Eel searched for its next
meal. Two hermit crabs scurried together upon the
ocean floor, and a school of small fish navigated
the sea in perfect synchronization.

Some of the creatures that swam by looked
curiously at us, not knowing what to make of this
bizarre scene: why was their home split down the
middle, and why were humans walking through?

The air was not only tinged with salt but
also seasoned with exhilaration. Sometimes we
would all sing songs together; other times we traveled in almost complete silence, wondering at the
miracle unfolding before our eyes. Most of the children let their hands drift through the water as they
walked by. A few younger brothers splashed their
sisters before being reproved by their parents.
Mothers pointed out unusual sea animals to their
fascinated sons, and some of the daughters were
propped up on their fathers' shoulders. The young
men cheered as exotic sea life drifted by, and the
young women exchanged astonished glances at

the humorous fish that floated around them. Older men who bore scars of Egyptian whips on their bodies looked at each other with tears in their eyes as if a great weight was suddenly lifted off their shoulders.

All through the night we marched between the glassy windows toward our freedom, the starry sky shimmering peacefully above us. I wished this waking dream would never end, but the hours flew by, and before we knew it, our destination came into view. We crossed over to the other side laughing and dancing. While we waited for the last of the group to arrive, we stood on the shore together to take in the final moments of the parted sea.

Then the miracle intensified.

The ocean's roar grew louder and a swarm of storm clouds began to rally overhead. They joined together to form a black veil, blanketing the stars in utter darkness. Dozens of scattered lightning bolts burst from above, and heavy rains fell from the clouds. The sky suddenly growled as if hungry for food, and the earth shook violently. The cries of horses sounded from afar, and the pillar of fire and cloud began spiraling like a tornado.

I looked at the storm above us, then at the tumultuous sea before us. I thought I saw something on the ocean's pathway, so I squinted through the tempest and inched towards the sea. I was able to discern horses . . . and chariots too!

The Egyptians had followed us through the sea!

For some reason they weren't getting any nearer, so I drew a bit closer to find out exactly what was happening. I saw soldiers clamoring in desperation, projecting their voices to be heard over the gale. Their chariots were stuck on the pathway, because the falling rain had churned the dry ground into mud. A soldier spotted me through the ocean mist and pointed me out to several of his comrades. I gazed on them steadily with my staff in hand. They looked at me, then at the storm engulfing them, and cried out with immediate comprehension, "Let's get out of here! The LORD is fighting for Israel against us!"

The Egyptians began panicking and frantically searching for a way of escape. The LORD spoke to me once more and said, "Raise your hand over the sea again. Then the waters will rush back over the Egyptian chariots and horsemen."

My eyes fell on the Egyptian army for the last time. They were once so terrifying, and now they were helpless creatures trapped between two soaring ocean walls. I lifted my hand without hesitation. The waters fell. It was as if God's invisible hands had been holding the watery barriers up all along, only to suddenly let go. The law of gravity was back in order, and the ocean collapsed to create the biggest splash I had ever seen. Every Israelite, now safely on shore, gaped at the helpless Egyptian army. The soldiers disappeared beneath the rumbling surge.

None survived. The world was silent.

The silence was broken when I felt a hand clasp my shoulder. I realized the world wasn't silent at all . . . only *my* world was, because ear-splitting Israelite cries of rejoicing gradually crept into my hearing. I looked behind me to find who the hand belonged to.

The burly man who had shouted angrily at me earlier was now clutching my shoulder. He looked at me through his tears and simply said, "Thank you, Moses."

The mother who had been weeping now had salty trails of joy on her cheeks. The panic-stricken man was lying on the shore with a grin of relief on his face.

Women began playing their tambourines. Children danced with reckless abandon. Fathers hoisted triumphant fists.

Everyone praised the LORD.

The skies began to clear. The sun pulled

itself over the horizon. The dark night of slavery had ended. The dawn of freedom had come.

I watched the Red Sea, now placid and quiet, and I understood. Now that I was on the other side, it all made sense. This sea had once been an obstacle, but it became the pathway of deliverance. It had once trapped us between itself and certain defeat, but it became the miracle that saved our lives. It had once left us for our enemies, but it became the very thing God used to destroy them.

I already knew that hardships were platforms for miracles.

But today, I understood that hardships are just miracles in disguise.

Nine

Worry's Dark Mirage

Do not worry.

This is one of the most challenging concepts for us to grasp. At any given moment there are a million different things we could worry about, because worry besieges the mind and attacks from all sides. With cunning precision, anxiety captures one thought at a time, summoning panic and fear from our untamed emotions to overthrow our already unstable peace. We are persuaded that fretting "isn't that big of a deal," so we let our guards down and fail to take our thoughts captive as the enemy opens fire and assaults our souls.

One of the most insidious tactics of the devil is to make us believe that worry is pointless, but certainly not dangerous. But worry is one of the deadliest weapons in his arsenal. It paralyzes us instantly, replacing our noble endeavors with needless inaction. It inhibits our growth and grows our inhibitions. It defers our hope and poisons our hearts. It cripples our passion and blinds our vision. Worry is venom and destruction hidden in a harmless exterior.

The most frequent and brutal blow this death-dealing weapon gives is the fear of tomorrow. The future can be one of the most terrifying prospects when overcast by the looming shadows of worry. When we fret about tomorrow, we are attempting to exist in a realm contrived by misguided thoughts and twisted imagination. The fear of the future allures us into a world that does not even exist, forcing our lungs to breathe the air of fallacy while our reality is overwhelmed by the theoretical. It diverts our focus to the tantalizing mirage down the road, compelling us to speculate about mere delusions.

That is why Jesus said, "Do not worry about tomorrow." The future rests safely in His promises, and the gift of the future is ours only after we open the present. The unwarranted pressure of what lies ahead is a burden that does not even belong to us. Of course, we might *feel* afraid about the future, but that is not real fear. Real fear has its victory only when we let our apprehensive emotions over-take our courageous endeavors. Real fear starts at our feelings, spreads to our choices, then cripples our actions. Fear tells us all the things we cannot do . . . but courage steps out and does them anyway. Courage is the resolve to refuse worry and to press on despite terror's paralyzing demands.

Be very courageous, and do not agonize about tomorrow. God has already prepared your fate. He will guide you to the Promised Land. His words will not fail you, and His presence will never abandon you. Dreading the future will only injure your purpose today.

But once we've defeated the fear of tomorrow, we must turn around to parry the surprise attack of yesterday. Paul the Apostle said, "I focus on this one thing: forgetting the past and looking forward to what lies ahead, I press on to reach the end of the race and receive the heavenly prize for which God, through Christ Jesus, is calling us." Jesus commanded us not to worry about tomorrow, and Paul furthered this mentality by stating that he chose to forget his past. He was running a race and had no time to get stuck in yesterday. His goal required him to forget about what was behind so that he could apprehend what lay ahead. He refused to let his yesterdays dictate his tomorrows. The past could not tyrannize him.

Paul's dream was to unfurl the standard of the Kingdom of God. He was adamant about leading others to salvation, but before he became a Christian he actually attempted to eradicate the Church. He aspired to extirpate Christianity, and the Bible says he breathed threats and murders against Jesus' disciples. Near the end of his life, he even called himself the chief of sinners. If anyone had a reason to be guilted by the past, it was Paul. He could have said, "Who am I to be used by Jesus? I'm the one who tried to destroy His work!" But he understood that Jesus' blood cleansed all of his sins. He understood that if he was to win the race and attain the heavenly prize, he had to keep running forward and leave yesterday behind.

The guilt of the past is a burden we are not designed to bear. God has erased our sins from His memory, He has cast them behind His back, and He has removed them as far away from us as the east is from the west. If God has put our sins behind Him, then shouldn't we do the same?

Our shameful past is now a testimony of God's redemption, because what Satan intended for evil, God uses for good. The devil is trapped in a perpetual lose-lose predicament, because God transforms even our worst losses into great victories. This is also true for the trials of the past. Yesterday's sorrows are tomorrow's strengths, and the lions and bears of the past help us face the giants today. Every great trouble serves an even greater future.

So don't be ensnared by the tragedy of the

past, but don't be a prisoner to the good memories of the past either. When we become nostalgic, reminiscing on days gone by and wishing things could be like they used to be, we will miss the gifts God desires to give us right now. When our wistful thoughts of memories long gone slowly transform into a debilitating longing for yesterday, today will slip through the cracks tragically unnoticed. The good times of the past should not depress us, they should excite us! Yesterday's memories are only a whisper of tomorrow's splendor.

The past should be the shoulders we stand upon, not a burden we carry on our shoulders. Don't be intimidated by yesterday, just jump on top of it. Grow with it. Yesterday will teach you to grow taller, and it will enable you to see further.

The psalmist said, "This is the day the Lord has made; we will rejoice and be glad in it." Our lives are not made up of the yesterdays or the tomorrows but of the todays. What we do today determines what tomorrow will be, and today's actions will determine if we've truly learned from yesterday's mistakes. The present is an exhilarating journey, because it is our current actions that build the future. Live fully for Jesus today, because you cannot get to tomorrow or improve on yesterday without it. We've never had this day before, and we will never have it again, so make it unforgettable.

Yesterday is a teacher. Tomorrow is a hope. But today is a choice, an opportunity to stand on the shoulders of a teacher that will carry us to the heights of hope.

Ten

Walking in the Miraculous

I opened my eyes to what seemed to be just another ordinary day as the sun crept across the sapphire sky. I awoke from under a nearby tree, crawled onto my mat, and was carried to my favorite spot right next to the gate called Beautiful. It was there, just outside the temple, that I made my living as a beggar.

I had never actually passed through the gate to enter the temple, because I felt I was too hideous a creature to ever seek the face of God.

How could He possibly love me?

Over the years my heart had become progressively bitter. I quickly was inured to poverty and hardship, so I simply concluded that God did not care for me.

I decided that I did not care much for Him either.

I only used God to employ my panhandling tactics. I would seek alms from those who went into the temple to seek Him. They had a reputation of helping the impoverished and disabled, and I would receive much from them . . . but it was never enough. The more money I received, the more unhappy I became. I was dependent on others for my needs, but they could not give what I really needed. I thought money was the answer, but it only managed to leave my heart bankrupt. I thought it was my stomach that needed filling when, in reality, it was my soul that was truly empty.

But what was I to do?

I was born crippled, and I am an only child. My parents always told me I was their 'pride and joy.' They made me feel so valuable and they treated me as if I was the best gift in all the world. They always cared for me and lavished their love upon me. But when they died, now many long years ago, all my love died with them. Love became to me a tormenting memory, a whisper of the past, haunting my mind and racking my soul. My parents' death burned like an inferno inside of me, until my heart became nothing more than ashes and dust. Day after day a festering shadow hovered over my ashes, leaking a growing bitterness into my nearly corroded thoughts. For years I was a captive locked behind the bars of my shame and desperation. With no one left to care for me, I resorted to begging.

But on that supposedly ordinary day, everything changed.

I wiped the sleep from my eyes (for I had quite a predisposition to sleeping in) and readied myself to begin my begging for the day right next to the Beautiful Gate.

"Have you any money to spare for an old cripple like myself?" I asked two men heading into the temple.

Simultaneously, they stopped dead in their tracks as if they heard the same inaudible command. Rarely did anyone completely stop for me, and I was really rather alarmed. They slowly turned their heads to face me.

Their countenances glowed with unfeigned joy. Their eyes locked onto mine. I was held captive in their gaze, and I could not escape such a wonderful imprisonment. I felt defenseless and vulnerable, while at the same time peacefully secure.

"We do not have silver or gold," I remember one of them saying.

We do not have silver or gold: words I'd heard a million times. Words that had commenced so many disappointing days. Words that, today, made me . . . well . . . *happy*. In their cheerful tone of voice I sensed they had something more than silver and gold. Something better.

"But what we do have," he continued, "we will give to you."

I felt a surge of power cascade down my body. It coursed through my veins and into my bones. The world around me seemed to freeze and, as if in slow motion, the man grabbed my right arm and lifted me up while boldly proclaiming, "In the name of Jesus Christ of Nazareth, rise up and walk!"

I landed on my two feet.

And . . . I did not fall.

Swift tears rolled down my cheeks.

"John! Peter!" I heard a voice call from the temple. "Come on, we are about to begin!"

Revelation dawned.

Peter and John, the famous disciples of Jesus, were standing right in front of me! Their names were on the lips of many and their miracles were published throughout the land, but I had never believed the reports. I scoffed in my heart at the stories I overheard from those coming in and out of the temple.

I remembered one occasion where a man and a woman had walked out of the temple and sat down together only a few paces from where I was lying. They told the story of a man named Peter, and how he had actually walked on water with

Jesus. But when Peter took his eyes off of Jesus, and looked instead at the tempest around him, he quickly began to sink. The man went on to tell how Jesus rescued Peter and calmed the wild storm.

The memory was still fresh in my mind.

That was Peter's very first time learning to walk on water, just as I would soon learn, for the very first time, to walk on land. Together, we would walk in the miraculous.

I looked into Peter's eyes, the same eyes that looked to Jesus and also turned away, and I understood. He gazed on me knowingly. His piercing eyes seemed to speak straight into my soul: *As you begin your walk, always remember, never take your eyes off Jesus.*

I nodded solemnly.

He smiled radiantly.

I looked down at my feet, put one foot in front of the other, and began to walk.

Suddenly, the bitterness and pain I harbored for so many years vanished from my heart, and never returned. I finally understood that even in spite of my delusions and misconceptions about God, He had always cared for me. His providence had prepared me for this moment. All along, He was patiently waiting for the right time to work and the right time to heal.

The shadow had passed. I looked up to the sun. I leapt with all my might and sang with all my heart.

As I walked through the Beautiful Gate, accompanied by Peter and John, I opened the gate of my heart, and Jesus gave me beauty for ashes. God touched me, and I was never the same. I entered the temple for the very first time, walking, leaping, and praising God.

Eleven

Overcoming Twilight

Sometimes the only way to move forward is to go back to the start.

When in your life were your prayers most fervent, your worship most passionate, your faith most daring? When did you reach the peak of that monumental mountaintop experience with God? When did your unassuming countenance reflect the Lord's shining face, and when were you more excited about Him than anything in the world?

Have the cares of life stifled the Word of God that once took root and flourished so freely? Have the inevitable hardships and suffering numbed your emotions and quenched your prospects? Have the difficult questions you can't yet answer overwhelmed the simple truths and breathtaking promises you once held so close?

Contrary to what you may have believed, your best days with God can start now. If you choose to, you can be closer to God today than you have ever been in the past. The Lord is waiting for you back where you first met.

The dawn can overcome the twilight. Patient years can restore youth. In the end, the beginning is the destination. Return to your first love.

Dig deep until you reach the foundation. Dismantle your questions and fears. Turn back to your home, and the Father will run to meet you. Trust like a small child in His accepting embrace, and plant your mustard seed of faith in the soil of His heart.

Revisit the world where imagination runs deep, where becoming a child is the aim of the wise. Explore the land where ambitions are noblest, where the servants are esteemed higher than all. Delve deep into the very veins of Heaven, where the blood of martyrs flows from the heart of Christ's passion, where death births life and the present meets eternity. Travel back to the womb of rebirth, and open wide the eyes of Christian existence. Reverse your momentum from rising up to kneeling down, and bow in the looming shadow of Calvary's wings. Fly through the infinite skies of forgiveness where east and west never meet. Immerse yourself in the heights and depths, length and width of divine, inseparable love. Recall the story of how God and man met when God became a man, and how an empty grave resurrected man's dying heart. Return to the promises that resound with a "yes" and "amen," and a belief that feeds on the words of God. Fall back to the poverty that makes rich and the weakness that makes strong.

Defeat your doubts with the faith you once grasped so tightly. Resume your pursuit of the knowledge of Jesus. Walk into the presence of God boldly. Reach higher than you ever dreamed of reaching. Now is your chance to arise to your earliest passion. His wings can bear you to the mountain's peak. Go back to the beginning, and move forward from there.

Twelve

Resurrected Belief

"Thomas, Thomas!" shouted the disciples as they hurried towards me. Their eyes were wild with anticipation, and a fierce joy radiated from each of their faces. I had never seen them so ecstatic.

What could they possibly be so happy about? Jesus was dead. And all that mattered died with Him. Without the Lord in my life, life had lost its meaning. For days I had been drowning alone in an ocean of tears, and I couldn't fathom what could possibly make the others so enthusiastic during such a time as this.

I wiped the tears from my eyes just before they skidded to a halt right in front of me. They bent over and put their hands on their knees to catch their breath.

"Thomas," Peter said between gasps. "We've been looking for you everywhere! You're not going to believe this . . . oh if you had only been there! I could hardly believe my eyes, and at first it seemed too good to be true but . . ."

"Peter!" said John, cutting off his sentence.

Peter had a tendency to ramble on and on when he was excited about something without ever really getting to the point, and John was usually the one to get him back on track.

"Right," agreed Peter, turning a little red. He looked around at the other disciples and gave them an energetic nod. Then, all at once, the disciples declared, "We have seen the Lord!"

My mouth fell to the floor. My breath avoided my lungs. I couldn't speak. A spark of impossible hope was kindled in my heart, and it quickly grew into a wild fire that consumed all my sorrow.

But the blazes vanished as quickly as they appeared. They were quenched by the rains of reason that began to fall from my mind into my heart. Like falling asleep after a miserable day, dreaming a wonderful dream, then waking to find cruel reality rush into consciousness, my hope crashed when confronted with the truth, the truth that Jesus was dead. Everyone knew that. The disciples couldn't have seen Him. It was simply impossible. Surely they had seen an apparition, or maybe even a vision, but there was no way they saw the Lord in the flesh as they supposed . . . there was just no way.

Lost in my thoughts, I hadn't yet given them a reply. Peter grabbed my shoulders impatiently and shook me as if to wake me out of shock. Staring straight into my eyes, he slowly said, "Thomas, the Lord is risen. He stood in our very midst. He is alive!"

Despite the unshakable confidence in his eyes, I just couldn't believe it. I wouldn't believe it. I had already been crushed by the Lord's death, and if they were wrong, my heart couldn't take being crushed all over again. The Lord was dead. There was nothing that would change that. Nothing could bring Jesus back.

Peter looked at me expectantly. The others stood behind him, also anxiously awaiting my response. A suspenseful silence hung in the air.

Finally, I opened my mouth to speak. "Unless I see the nail marks in His hands," I demanded, "and put my finger where the nails were, and put my hand into His side, I will not believe it."

Eight days later

We'd been praying for nearly an hour. We were huddled together in the upper room we used as our secret meeting place, the very spot in which the others claimed to see the Lord. But I still hadn't seen the Savior, and the test of time seemed to show that my doubts were proving true after all.

Echoes of agreement filled the chamber as Phillip lifted up a heartfelt prayer. It seemed like each disciple was lost in the presence of God . . . except for me. Whenever it came my turn to pray aloud, I found I just didn't have much to say. I was unable to draw fervor from my heart because everything inside me felt hollow. I was hurting. Everything I ever was had been shattered at the cross. The others were more on fire for the Lord than ever, but my spirit wandered under the starless sky of a never-ending night. I reeled amidst the darkness, and I wondered if the sun would ever rise.

Phillip concluded his prayer, we all said "amen," then we opened our eyes. I lifted my head and . . . I couldn't believe what I saw.

Jesus.

It can't be. It just can't be, I thought to myself.

He looked at each of our faces, one by one, then said, "Peace be with you!"

All my doubt fled at the sound of His voice. The flames of hope began to burn in my soul once again, and this time I knew nothing in the world could quench them. The risen Son dethroned the dark night that had tyrannized my spirit.

At last the dawn had come.

The Son walked over to me with a powerful smile that warmed my heart. His eyes seemed to glow as He looked on me. A blissful, child-like innocence radiated from His gaze, yet somewhere behind His eyes I could sense unmistakable memories of pain. My sense was confirmed when I noticed the one thing about Him that had changed.

There were scars on His body.

"Put your finger here," He said to me, "and see My hands. Put your hand into the wound in My side. Do not be unbelieving, but believing."

I dropped to my knees. Two streams of tears fell silently down my face. I touched His wounds and cried, "My Lord and my God!"

His loving gaze remained firm on me as He said, "Thomas, because you have seen Me, you have believed. Blessed are those who have not seen and yet have believed."

My heart broke. An overpowering sense of guilt stained my mind. How could I have doubted my Savior? How could I have lost hope in the One who died for me?

But as I looked again at His wounds, I remembered the blood of the new covenant that flowed from them. I reached out my hand, and the moment I touched His wounds again, my own were healed. His blood flooded all that I was and swept away my guilt.

My resurrected faith soared through the skies of redemption. I basked in the Son's healing wings. I renewed my pledge to my King as I knelt on the ground, and my heart was raised high as I bowed low before Him. Jesus had waged war on the grave, and He emerged victorious. His tomb was empty so that my heart could be filled.

Behold, my Redeemer lives.

Thirteen

Divided Hearts Will Break

Our generation is falling prey to the tyrants of fear because we are falling away from the fear of God.

There is no meaning to our existence where the fear of the Lord is nonexistent. Life cannot be reborn without death to self, and a harvest of salvation is evidenced by fruits of repentance. The choices we make are crucial steps in the race of our lives toward the Kingdom of God, and if we base every decision on the fact that we carry Jesus with us everywhere we go, we will apprehend our heavenly prize. Our awareness of the Lord's presence will compel us to abhor the evil that would destroy us and cling to the good that reflects our redemption.

Jesus said that we are His friends if we obey Him, and the Bible says that loving God means keeping His commandments. Jesus' love is so vehement that He hugged His cross so we can live in His embrace, and His friendship deserves our deepest awe and most staunch dedication. But if we say we are His friends, yet our lives defy His ways, then we are deluding ourselves. And if we say that our faith is in God, but we cannot demonstrate our belief with good deeds, then our faith is dead. Real faith is not a mere intellectual belief in God, but a heart-felt belief in Him that births action and change.

Jesus said to the Church of Laodicea in the book of Revelation that He would spit them out of His mouth because they were neither hot nor cold. If half of our life is devoted to God, but the other half is devoted to the world's system, we cannot experience the fullness of God. To be a friend of the world is to be an enemy of God. We can never fully submit to two masters: neither will get all of our attention, and each will receive only half of our heart. If our heart is divided, at war against itself, both sides will lose.

Divided hearts always break.

The heart's victory can be secured only after it has ventured the pathway of surrender. You will discover freedom once you chain yourself to Christ, while the liberty the world offers ends only in chains. You will find your courage embedded in your fear of the Lord, and your rewards in Heaven hide within your obedience on earth. But sin guides to certain death. It lures us with fleeting pleasures and leaves us with permanent scars. It drives us from God, creating an impossible chasm that severs our lives from His.

Jesus' cross is the only bridge we can walk to cross that gap. His blood can destroy our lingering depravity, and His Spirit can breathe new life into our lungs. Our tears of repentance will water the seeds of redemption He has planted inside of our hearts, and our lives will flourish as we bask in the Son of God. The fruit of our faith will feed minds that are starved by doubt, and the living water that flows from our actions will bring revival to souls that are dying. Our fear of the Lord will replace our fears in life, and our wholehearted devotion will lay waste to the walls that divide our hearts.

The Light of the World has invaded the shadows that have enslaved us. Sin no longer has dominion over us. At last the gaze of our souls locks onto redemption. At last we are free.

Fourteen

Perceiving the Unseen

Under the canopy of a starry sky, a sea of Syrian warriors stood silently around the city of Dothan, preparing themselves to strike. Soon they would crash upon Elisha like a tidal wave. He was surrounded. Impossibly outnumbered. There would be no chance for escape.

But there was something the Syrian army forgot to factor into their equation . . .

God.

It was early in the morning. The sun began to climb over the hills of Dothan. I rolled out of bed yawning, stretched out my arms, and grabbed the pitcher to fetch water for the day. I took one step outside and halted as if I had run into an invisible wall. My pitcher fell from my numb fingers as I gawked at the army of Syrian raiders less than fifty paces from where I was standing. They were all staring right at me. I froze under their icy gazes. My heart was racing, but I couldn't get my feet to move. For what seemed a lifetime, I was unable to flee, but when my senses finally kicked in I ran back inside to the temporary safety of our lodgings.

Elisha was sitting on his favorite chair with his head bowed in prayer. I hurried over to him, fell to my knees, and cried, "Ah, my lord, what will we do now?"

He looked down at me. An unwavering calm was in his eyes. He didn't reply immediately but instead rose to his feet and walked to the doorway. Like a general studying his enemy just before battle, Elisha looked steadily out upon the Syrian army. He watched quietly for a moment, then shifted to face me. A smile slid onto his face, and I realized he knew something I didn't. He slowly made his way towards me, extended his hand, and helped me to my feet. He squeezed my shoulder and said firmly, "Do not be afraid! For there are more on our side than on theirs!"

Had my master lost his senses? There were only two of us! What could he possibly mean, "there are more on our side than on theirs"?

He gestured a hand toward the entryway, beckoning me to take another look outside. I peered out and examined the enemy, but nothing seemed to have changed. I turned back to Elisha and, seeing my puzzled expression, he lifted his gaze and humbly prayed, "O LORD, open his eyes and let him see!"

A sudden tingling sensation tickled my eyes. I shut them, lowered my head, then rubbed them for a moment. When the tingling had vanished, I opened my eyes again. I brought my head up . . . and I couldn't believe what I saw.

The hillside around us was filled with an army of angels. The heavenly warriors were perfect beings. They were tall, fair-skinned, and brawny. A faint glow emitted from their slightly transparent bodies, and each was garbed in armor of white light. Fiery intricacies were emblazoned on the breast-plates. A small star glistened on the forehead of their helms. Opalescent vambraces were wrapped around their wrists, and golden sandals twined up their shins. Most sat on the backs of luminous horses or rode in chariots made of fire, but the remaining footmen formed perfectly disciplined ranks. The front line held long, silver spears. In the middle column, each held an oblong shield in one hand and wielded a blazing sword in the other. Behind them, in the final row, the archers patiently held strange black arrows on the string of each of their bows.

I stared at the army with a quickened pulse while holding a sharp intake of breath. This reality surpassed my wildest imagination, and my captivated mind just couldn't wrap itself around this magnificent moment. I rubbed my eyes once more, but when I opened them again the divine warriors were still there!

The Syrians, however, were oblivious to the angelic host. They marched in our direction, but now that my eyes were opened to the heavenly army, I was no longer fearful.

As the enemy drew nearer, Elisha bowed his head and clasped his hands together. "O LORD," he prayed, "please make them blind."

Just then, a rank of archers in the angelic army fired the strange black arrows at the Syrians' faces. With perfect precision, each invisible dart connected with its target. Suddenly blinded, the Syrians grabbed at their eyes and scrunched their faces together. As if in a drunken stupor they wobbled back and forth, waving one hand in front of their faces as if they could somehow bat away the darkness like flies. The arrows must have been a special weapon, striking any foe with sudden blindness.

Elisha walked toward them and shouted, "You have come the wrong way! This isn't the right city! Follow me, and I will take you to the man you are looking for."

Bewildered and at a loss for words, the

Syrian captains took several staggered steps in Elisha's direction. Falling for the prophet's ruse, they nodded their heads and agreed to follow. They weren't about to give up on their mission to capture Elisha, even though they had just been smitten by the mysterious blindness. They couldn't afford to come back to their king empty-handed. There was no possibility of Syria ever winning the war against Israel with Elisha still on the loose. Because of divine revelation, the man of God was able to predict where the Syrian forces would mobilize next. He had warned King Jehoram about the impending attacks, thus enabling Israel to escape ambush. Elisha was a hindrance that needed to be removed if Syria was to be victorious.

I hastened to Elisha's side as he led the Syrian host away from Dothan. The heavenly army surrounding us gradually began to fade. In a matter of moments, they had vanished completely. They had accomplished their mission. Their work here was done.

Elisha walked only several paces ahead of the Syrian army, directing them by audible commands. When we finally approached our destination, Elisha looked at me with a crafty grin. I nearly let out a cry of triumph as comprehension dawned. He was leading them into the perfect trap. The city walls of Samaria loomed above us . . . he was leading the army to the capital city of Israel!

They had attempted to take Elisha captive, but now they were about to be the captives.

A battalion of Israelite troops was waiting for us just outside the city walls. Once inside, Elisha ordered the Syrians to halt. He squeezed his eyes shut, clenched his hands, and prayed, "O LORD, now open their eyes and let them see."

The Syrians shouted jubilantly as their sight returned. But in only several seconds their cheers turned to murmurs of bemusement and dismay upon the realization that they were in Samaria, encircled by Israelite troops. Now painfully aware that Elisha had deceived them, they looked at each other, shook their heads, and raised their hands in surrender.

Right then, King Jehoram came running out to see the captured army. He was smiling from ear to ear, and he had to hold his crown to keep it from falling off as he hurried excitedly toward us. With large, beaming eyes he looked on his new prisoners, then turned to Elisha and asked, "My father, should I kill them?"

"Of course not!" Elisha answered. "Do we kill prisoners of war?" He paused in silent consideration to glance at the captives before continuing,

"Give them food and drink and send them home again to their master."

The king blinked in astonishment. He chewed on his lower lip pensively, then smiled, let out a sigh, and nodded his head slowly. He was clearly awed by Elisha's greatness and wisdom, and his expression unveiled the deep admiration he felt for the man of God.

Adhering to Elisha's command, Jehoram prepared a meal fit for a king for each of the captured soldiers, then sent them back to their home.

So the bands of Syrian raiders came no more into the land of Israel.

Fifteen

Fighting for Harmony

A kingdom divided against itself cannot stand. We cannot achieve victory over our enemy if we are waging war on each other. How can we become fishers of men if our time is spent casting judgment on one another?

We are in desperate need of unity in the Church today.

We are a song that can inspire the world, if we will live our lives together in harmony. We can be a dazzling symphony, a melodious orchestration of flutes and violins, trumpets and drums, when we accompany faithfulness to play our part with a respect for the distinctive contribution of others. We will arrest the imagination of the world as our voices fuse into anthems of kindness and melodies of forgiveness. We will brandish the banner of peace and love, and we will unify in Jesus' name alone.

We are the Body of Christ, the physical representation of Jesus Himself. We are hands to build the Kingdom of Heaven and feet to run the Good

News to the world. We are eyes to perceive visions of change and ears to hear the cries of the needy. It is our mission to accurately portray His image. We are the mirror of Heaven, reflecting His beauty and grace to a world of shattered hearts. Before the Lord was crucified, He prayed that His followers would be one . . . now it is up to us to realize His dream. But have we let disparate denominations, political affiliations, differing perspectives, and contrastive lifestyles divide us? Have we relinquished our purpose just to pick sides and pick fights?

We need each other. Each member of the Body is required in order to properly depict who Jesus is. The Lord has rigorously designed you to meet the purpose He has so delicately prepared for you. You are fearfully and wonderfully made, and your qualities give vitality to the Body of Christ. God has created you perfectly for your dreams and He has fashioned you specially for His plans, and without your contribution, the Body just won't be the same. So be the best version of yourself. The Body needs you.

And you need the Body. The feet need the hands to do the work, and the hands need the feet to travel to the place where the work needs to be done. Without each other, we are incomplete. Our strengths and weaknesses are puzzle pieces fitting together to show the world the big picture. If one piece is missing, the picture will be confusing and partial. And the detached missing piece will lose its value if it tries to survive alone. We each play a crucial part, and we will not thrive if we all try to make it on our own. We must stick together, or we will all fall apart.

Each one of us is unique, so we will naturally have differences. But our differences were not meant to destroy unity, but to birth versatility. We all wear the same jersey, and every role is vital. But so many people refuse Christianity because they watch us combat each other. They already fight daily battles within and without, and they have no strength for the civil war of the Church. They shudder at the thought of our judgmental attitudes and barbaric conduct despite our 'ideology of love.' Judgmental warfare is a self-defeating conflict. It is a toxin pervading the Body of Christ, and it is up to us to destroy it before it destroys us. Besides, how can we judge others for the speck in their eye when we have a massive log in our own? Christ's body was broken two thousand years ago so that the Body of Christ could be made whole today.

Unity starts with us. It is high time to rid ourselves of the discord that has kept our triumph at bay. We can break free of cliques and boundaries.

Our unconventional friendships can dethrone the status quo. We will convey Jesus to the world by our love for one another, and because we are one, the lost will be won. We will be a refuge for souls abandoned by their broken families, and we will extend peace to those who have known only war. We will fight for harmony. We will know victory. The gates of hell will never prevail against us.

Sixteen

Captive Liberty

Paul and I sat in the gloom of a Philippian dungeon. Our feet were fastened in the stocks. Multiple trails of dried blood streaked down both of our backs. A throbbing, unrelenting pain tormented my body. The engulfing shadows crept into the deep chambers of my mind. We looked at each other with weary eyes. The burden apparent in Paul's gaze made him look ten years older than he did only a day before.

This was where our adventures had led us.

Paul had just cast a demon out of a slave girl and, because she brought her masters much profit by fortune telling, they were infuriated when she lost her dark ability. Their hopes of wealth were shattered, so they dragged us into the marketplace to the authorities. The whole city was in an uproar because of our Gospel message, and we were indicted for teaching people to do things against Roman customs. A mob quickly formed against us, and the magistrates ordered that we be stripped and beaten with wooden rods. After our beating we were cast into the inner dungeon where the most dangerous criminals were to be caged.

But I refused the pointlessness of just lying in the cold shadows, sulking in despair. The unseen presence of the One we gladly suffered for was right in the cell with us. Although the outer gloom was patiently fighting its way into my mind, I found strength meditating on the coming day when I would be sitting in a mansion of white light, able to see my Lord face to face. We would feast and talk and laugh, and I would worship Him with all of my might.

Yet I realized I could worship Him with all of my might *right now*. Whether caged in a dungeon of darkness, or feasting at the future table of Jesus in the Kingdom of Light, either way, I could praise Him with my whole heart. Worship is a choice.

And I chose to worship.

Who ever said a prison cell can't be turned into a sanctuary?

I looked over at Paul. He managed a faint, yet heartfelt, smile and said in a strained voice, "Blessed are you when you're persecuted for righteousness' sake. Rejoice and be exceedingly glad, for great is your reward in Heaven."

. . . the promise of our Lord.

Jesus' assurances always fortified the walls

of my strength. They obviously gave Paul strength in that moment as well because his smile grew a lot bigger, and he nodded at me as if to say, "Silas, you know what to do."

I smiled back knowingly.

Simultaneously, we lifted our voices together and worshipped the Lord. I closed my eyes, focused my mind, and channeled all the passion of my heart into song. Despite the darkness that surrounded us, the light of the Lord seemed to swell inside of us. We began to sing louder and louder, garnering strength from somewhere beyond ourselves. We turned to the Stronghold as prisoners of hope . . . as prisoners of Christ . . . and I was free.

Paul always liked to say, "Where the Spirit of the Lord is, there is liberty." And ironically, this was made clear to me while I was a prisoner. The shackles of my soul were breaking, and I was captivated by the evident presence of Jesus.

My thoughts ascended beyond my cell. I forgot about the pain. The darkness that tried to creep into me shriveled up and cowered in retreat. I soared into Heaven on eagles' wings. My strength was rising as I waited upon Him. I submerged my soul in the joy of the Lord, and my voice couldn't even come close to reaching the zenith of passion I felt in my heart.

I had never experienced such a beautiful time of worship.

I'm not sure how long we were singing. Minutes? Hours? It's easy to lose track of time when you're caught up in the timeless presence of God, but I was pulled back down to reality when several disgruntled protests came from some of the prisoners. It was the middle of the night, and we didn't necessarily have the best singing voices, so I could hardly blame them. They were all listening to us, and although I never felt comfortable singing in front of others, I was surprisingly unabashed. I'm sure a number of them thought we were deranged, seeing that we spent our first night in the dungeon (after having been severely beaten) singing cheerful hymns. Others must have been slightly entertained. But those who were trying to sleep were not too happy to be awakened by our inharmonious singing at this time of the night.

We quieted our voices momentarily to relocate our zeal from song to prayer. With supplication and thanksgiving, we made our requests known to God. We prayed that every single prisoner would witness the display of God's power. We interceded on behalf of friends back home. We petitioned for salvation to come to many souls in Philippi, and beseeched the Father to show Himself strong by performing a miracle even in this very dungeon. Even tonight.

Then we began to sing some more.

All of a sudden, there was a faint rumble beneath our feet. The rumble grew louder, increasing in intensity, until the whole world seemed to shake violently. The prison doors burst open. Fetters fell off of the prisoners' feet. The stocks shook loose. Euphoric shouts of freedom rose above the roar of the tremor.

And the earth stood still.

At least, it *seemed* to stand still because the earthquake vanished as quickly as it came. An immediate, quiet peace lingered in the air. The prisoners stood motionless, gazing at us with wide eyes as if we were the source of this great phenomenon.

From the corner of my eye, I caught a glimpse of the jailor who had just woken up. He looked around at the yawning prison doors. Terror swept across his face. He drew out his sword, aimed the blade at his stomach, and was about to thrust.

"Don't do it!" Paul shouted desperately. "We are all here!"

The jailor stared at Paul. His hands didn't move. He waited for what seemed a lifetime.

He dropped his blade.

Its loud clank on the hard floor echoed dramatically. Still trembling in fear, he called out to a nearby servant to bring him light. A young man ran in with two torches in hand and led the jailor to our cell. With wonder in their eyes, they hurried past the newly freed prisoners who inexplicably lingered by their fallen chains. The jailor arrived huffing and puffing and, overwhelmed, he fell down at our feet.

He rose up, clasped both of our hands, and guided us out of the dungeon.

"Sirs," he asked through teary eyes, "what must I do to be saved?"

"Believe on the Lord Jesus Christ," I said.

Paul grabbed his shoulder, adding, "And you and your household shall be saved."

The tears piling in his eyes fell instantly, streaming down his cheeks. Hope gleamed in his gaze. The other prisoners gathered around us. They still weren't ready to flee. They were too eager to hear about the Savior who could set captives free. So we preached the Gospel to our captive audience, then Paul and I sang another song to Jesus.

And this time, no one told us to be quiet.

Seventeen

Unlocking the Fervor of Praise

Every breath is a miracle, so cherish each one as an opportunity to love the God who gives you life. Worship Him today as if it were your very last chance here on earth. Employ your mind to create declarations of glory, and exploit the passion inside of your heart to present your deepest affection. Praise Him with child-like sincerity, and honor Him with your purest fervor. Believe in the reality of His presence, and seek His face and beauty with all the strength you can muster.

Bravely approach His throne, and take delight in the praises that you bring. Relinquish every distraction. Align your thoughts with His fathomless greatness. Ignite Heaven's wonders as you soar through the stars of promise and grace. Rejoice in the Father of lights, and turn back to offer grateful praise after every good and perfect gift. Send your choir to the front lines of the battle, and open up the prison doors with songs of faith. Discover the strength He hides deep within your weakness, and capture the dazzling honors instilled in the quietness of humility.

The glories of God are infinite, and there are so many treasures we have yet to unearth. When we worship the Lord, we dig up the riches of grace He has planted inside our very souls. Praise makes us part of something greater than ourselves. It unites us with all the citizens of Heaven, and it breaks down the walls that divide us. It solidifies our faith and eliminates the doubt that plagues us. It enables our vision to witness Christ's beauty and unveils the truth that sets us free. It is the fulfillment of our purpose and the inspiration of our love.

Our existence finds its meaning when we worship God, because we were created for His pleasure. His melody is music for our ears, and His beauties are the focus of our eyes. His countenance is a light for our step, and His mighty acts are the words on our lips. His promises are skies for our wings and His praise is the air that we breathe. His glory is the world we were destined to inhabit, so when we boast or complain or put idols before Him, we are attempting to exist in a world that is not created for us . . . a world we cannot survive in. But when God is first in our lives, when we glorify Him with all of our passions, we will blossom and grow into the beautiful, glowing creatures He has destined us to be.

Whenever you are about to complain, say something amazing about the Lord instead. When you are tempted to boast, shine the spotlight on God's accomplishments. When you feel apathy's iron grip but you just can't seem to feel God's touch upon your heart, lift your hands and touch His heart with a devoted sacrifice of praise. When your mind meanders through the abyss of futility and distraction, capture your thoughts and lead them to the marvelous light. When the unnerving darkness of despair envelops you, radiate your thanksgiving into the night and hope for the imminent dawn.

Your heart will be filled when you pour it out in worship. Your actions will be ignited when your song is on fire. Your purpose will be raised high when your soul bows low before the living God. Because in the end, you will never regret praising God too passionately, you will only regret not praising Him passionately enough.

Eighteen

Leprous Conceit

My name was on everyone's lips. The spreading of my fame could not be stopped. I was, to be sure, the greatest king of all time.

But I needed to be more than a king. I wanted to do something that no descendant of Israel had ever done before. David had been a prophet and a king, and Samuel had been a priest and a prophet, but never before had there been a king who was a priest. Sure, it was forbidden in God's law . . . but I was an exception.

God would be glad to bend the rules for me.

I mean, look at me. I was Uzziah, the beloved ruler whose accomplishments others attain only in their wildest dreams. I ascended to my throne at the young age of sixteen, and since then my success had been matchless. I'd amassed an indomitable military, vanquished all my foes, and utilized my agricultural expertise to help generate national prosperity. It's no wonder why I was the most renowned man in all the land.

But it was time for me to take my greatness to another level. It was time to secure my place in history.

With a censer in hand and a head held high, I sauntered into the temple sanctuary and loomed above the altar of incense. I closed my eyes to relish my emergence as Judah's very first priest-king. The significance of the moment sent shivers down my spine. For my first act as priest, I burned the incense and swung it before the altar. I breathed deeply as the sweet aroma permeated the air. But I was startled out of reverie when a voice cried, "My king, do not do this!"

Who could possibly have the audacity to barge into the sanctuary during my private ceremony? I turned to find the man to whom the voice belonged, and there stood Azariah the high priest. But he was not alone. Eighty other priests stood firm behind him with arms crossed. They stared at me with indignant eyes. I stared back. Our minds were engaged in silent warfare, but Azariah's low-pitched voice finally brought an end to the battle. "It is not right for you, Uzziah," he said, "to burn incense to the LORD. That is for the priests, the descendants of Aaron, who have been consecrated to burn incense. Get out of the sanctuary, for you have been unfaithful. The LORD God will not honor you for this!"

A black storm of fury raged within my heart. My blood boiled and rushed to my head. My hair stood on end. I clenched my fists and glared maliciously at the intruders. Who were these fools to deny me my great honor? I was the king! They had no right to order me around like that. How dare they challenge Uzziah the Great! They couldn't stop me.

No one could stop me.

I tightened my grip on the censer and continued swinging it defiantly before the altar of incense. I shook my head at the so-called priests and laughed proudly, but my cackling was promptly cut off by the sound of gasps. The priests took a step back and gaped at me with horrified expressions. I looked at them questioningly, and one of the speechless priests slowly lifted his hand and pointed at my forehead. I pressed my fingers to my forehead and felt a boil forming on my skin. Sudden rashes, boils, and shiny patches began to appear on my arms. I knew these symptoms . . .

Leprosy.

The censer fell from my hand. I stood blinking. I had to get out of the temple . . . I had to get out right away. The priests agreed. They rushed me outside, banning me from the house of the LORD.

For the rest of my days I would be consumed by a living death . . .

Ten years have passed since that horrendous day. Now I live in isolation and, as a leper, I am not allowed admittance into the temple ever again. My disease has pervaded my system and slowly eats me alive. My face is covered in permanent boils, my eyes are glazed over, lesions have infiltrated my arms, and all my fingers have transformed into nothing more than protruding stubs. I could hardly be called human any longer. I am a mutilated man displaying the physical manifestation of pride.

Although I cannot be cured of leprosy, I have been cured of the even more devastating disease of conceit. My body deteriorates, but my soul heals. I have found God again. In the days of my youth I sought after the LORD with fervor and devotion, but when I grew powerful my heart was lifted up. I didn't understand that all the success I enjoyed was a gift sent to me from God. I never earned any of His blessings. But my malady has drawn my heart back to the LORD, and the lowlier I become the higher my love for Him grows. It is better to be a humble leper than a proud king. My life has found meaning once again, because I know my tragic condition can rescue others from pride before they end up like me.

Nineteen

The Heart's Mirror

Out of the abundance of the heart the mouth speaks.

If we desire to see the true appearance of our own hearts, all we have to do is listen to the words we speak. Our hearts contain whatever we fill them with: what we watch with our eyes and listen to with our ears will flow down into their depths, and only those who pour purity into their hearts will be able to truly see God. If we pour in immorality, there will be no room for God. But when we take in God's words, they will come out of our mouths. Our conversations reflect our hearts, and they can either piece together or break the hearts of others. Each of us will give an account before God for what we've spoken, and if we do not think before we speak, our mindless words will become our deepest regrets.

Every conversation is significant because there isn't a single one that hasn't reached the ears of the Lord. Sin is always present in a multitude of words, so we would be wise to let them be few. When we lessen the amount of our words, we increase their value. Take your thoughts captive before they escape your mind and flee through your mouth. Speak up on behalf of those being gossiped about, instead of using your tongue to join in the slander. Attribute every good and perfect gift to God's name alone, and never boast about your own accomplishments. Don't repeat the lackluster, empty clichés, but give voice to only what you really believe. If you can't find the truth in what you're about to speak, then don't say it. Our discretion will inspire others to listen intently to the truths we share and the questions we ask. Pronounce life into the world around you.

Any fool can voice his opinion, but the wise man will hear what others have to say. Be swift to hear, and slow to speak, because oftentimes your ears can actually bring greater healing than your mouth. People long to be heard, but we cannot listen to them when the only voice we hear is our own. People frequently fix their problems by simply having someone who will listen to them talk, because many answers hide in their hearts and will often come out through their mouths. Hear each person intently and sincerely, as though they're the most important person in the world, because that's the attention God gives to us. Sometimes listening is more an act of giving than speaking is. Good listening is one of the greatest talents in the world, and it's a skill that any one of us can master.

Consider your words, because the power of life and death is in the tongue. The weight of your words can either make others stronger or be a weight their already-burdened shoulders have to bear. If anger wells up inside of you, close your mouth and wait patiently no matter how much it burns. When you are nervous but a door is opened for the preaching of the Gospel, open your mouth and fearlessly declare Christ's message. The easy half-truths are tempting, but remember that holiness is found only in the whole truth. Sorrow will seek its outlet through complaining, so capture your thought and transform it into a word of prayer. Doubt may seek to apprehend your soul, driving you to despair, but iterate the promises of God. When you are wronged and a vengeful remark seems justifiable, bless, and curse not.

You will discover what's inside of you when you listen to what comes out of you: your words are the mirror of your heart.

Twenty

Amongst My Heroes

I was so young. So inexperienced. So unqual-
ified.

I was just twenty years old . . .

It was a majestic morning. Scattered pink
clouds leisurely drifted above me. A soft golden
glow lay over the dewy blades of grass as the sun
prepared itself to soar through the sky for another
day. I sat with my back against a strong tree trunk
and rested my feet on its gnarled roots. The high,
twisting branches overhead covered me in perfect
shade while I observed the distant mountains.

This was my favorite spot to rest and
contemplate. It never ceased to amaze me what
spectacular insights a quiet mind could bring. I
was ready to hear from the LORD.

I had my scroll open in my lap to the passage
of Moses and the fiery bush. This was one of my
favorite stories. After forty years as a shepherd
in the desert, the LORD gave Moses a mission to
rescue the children of Israel. He was slow of speech
and tongue, yet God trained him to speak His word,

and now Moses' message is etched in history. The LORD used this simple man to divide an ocean, summon water out of a desert rock, convey the law while his face was illuminated, defeat an army by merely lifting his hands, and deliver an entire nation from four hundred years of slavery.

When it came to the tales of the prophets, I just couldn't get enough! My dreams awakened every time I would read about them. They were ordinary people, but they did extraordinary things for God.

I thought back to the prophet David. He was only a boy when he was anointed to be the future king of Israel, and God exalted him to one of history's greatest heroes. He was a gallant warrior who felled a giant with a sling and stone, a master musician who invented new instruments, an ardent poet who disclosed the heart of God with his pen, and a legendary king who subdued nations. God Himself called David a man after His own heart, and the zeal that flowed from his heart into the psalms never ceases to sing to the deepest chambers of my soul.

And, of course, there was Samuel. His life was born through the prayer of his once-barren mother Hannah. He was a prophet, priest, and Israel's final and most crucial judge. He uttered his first prophecy when he was only a child—and that was in a day when the word of the LORD was virtually nowhere to be found! He grew up serving the high priest in the tabernacle, faithful with the few things set before him, and God raised him up to change history when he helped transition the day of the judges to the reign of the kings.

And I couldn't forget about Isaiah. He walked around naked for three years as a symbol of the terror that would befall Egypt and Ethiopia. And then there was Jonah, the stubborn prophet who spent three days and nights in the belly of a fish before ushering Nineveh into one of history's greatest revivals. I was probably most impressed, though, by the bravely obedient Hosea who married a prostitute to portray God's love toward His unfaithful people. And the prophet Amos gave me hope because he was only a shepherd and tender of sycamore trees, but he was given God's oracles and wisdom to declare the future of the nation Israel.

The prophets were so devoted. They would do anything the LORD asked them to, even if it meant sacrificing their own names to glorify His.

All of a sudden, from out of nowhere, as I was ruminating on these truths, a miracle took place.

The Word of the LORD came to *me* . . .

Just like it did to all of my heroes!

I was expecting to hear from the LORD through the Scriptures. Not audibly! This was a wonder I would never forget. I couldn't believe the first thing God said to me:

"I knew you before I formed you in your mother's womb. Before you were born I set you apart and appointed you as My prophet to the nations."

Me? Could He really be talking to me? Surely this must have been some sort of mistake. I wasn't worthy to have my name on the list of all my heroes! I was too young, and far too ill-prepared.

"Ah, Lord God!" I said, "Behold, I cannot speak, for I am a youth."

Sure, I knew God used ordinary people to do extraordinary things. But *me*? That's an entirely different story. I didn't have what it would take to proclaim God's Word. I didn't have the wisdom. Or the training. Besides, who would ever listen to what I had to say? And how would I even *know* what to say? I mean, maybe the LORD would speak through me in the future . . . *maybe* . . . like twenty years from now!

But the LORD replied in a gentle yet emphatic tone, "Do not say, 'I am a youth,' for you shall go to all to whom I send you, and whatever I command you, you shall speak. Do not be afraid of their faces, for I am with you to deliver you."

The LORD reached out His invisible hand and touched my mouth. I felt a sudden torrent of power rush through my entire being. It cascaded from my head down to my feet, coursing through my veins. His Word was impressed on my tongue and burned in my very bones! It seemed nothing could stop it from coming out.

"Now I have put My words in your mouth," He said. "See, today I appoint you over the nations and kingdoms to uproot and to tear down, to destroy and to overthrow, to build and to plant."

His promise engulfed my soul. His Word had equipped my lips. I no longer felt young. Or afraid. Just empowered. And sure.

Sure that God really *can* use anyone . . .

Because He was about to use me.

I, Jeremiah, was about to speak God's Word to the nations.

Twenty-One

Beaming Hope to the Nations

Church, we must wake up. The world needs us, and our time is running out. Jesus is coming back soon, and we must stand now while we still have the chance. God's Word is hidden in our hearts, but not all things that are hidden should be kept secret. The world is thirsting for real change and genuine love. We can give that to them, if we will tear down the walls that divide us to build up the truth instead. But the world won't hear the truth of our words unless they discover the truth in our actions. They know that we believe in God, but is our faith real, or merely a substitute for good works? They know that we trust in God, but are we truly trusting in Him, or just letting Him do all the work while we sit back and do nothing? They know that we are waiting for the Lord, but are we waiting obediently, or is "patience" a mask we wear so we don't have to face the reality of our laziness?

The world is not looking for beliefs founded

on laziness, but actions founded on beliefs. Are we radiating Christ into the darkness, or have we condemned the darkness with our words while condoning it with our actions? Will we change reality, or will we let reality change us? Our good deeds can illuminate the pathway for the souls that stagger in the shadows. We are bright lights, illustrating the hope of Heaven by the lives we lead. As a picture speaks a thousand words, so our good deeds paint the reality of eternity more than our words ever could. When the world sees our faith evidenced in our lifestyles, they will listen to our burning message.

Our greatest calling is not to tell the world our stance on issues, but to walk on the path of love. We must act on our beliefs if we want to direct souls to Christ. The Lord teaches us to love, but the Bible also teaches that He *is* love. He has taught us the truth, but He also *is* the truth. Jesus always lived what He believed, and His conduct always aligned with His convictions. We believe it is good to help the poor, so let's help them! We want to see people saved, so let's be creative and find ways to evangelize. We know immorality will destroy us, so let's put our whole hearts into leading godly lives as we follow after the Spirit. We can give others the riches of God's grace if we will seize the golden opportunities before us.

Everyone has perspectives, and perspectives rarely change things. People are searching for the reality of truth in the lives of those who believe it. Truth is not a front to hide behind: it's a way of living. Our generation is chasing after the truth, and if our lifestyles don't match our convictions, they will look for truth somewhere else. We have the power to guide the lost to our Heavenly home, but if our lifestyles counter our claims, we will only drive home the void and confusion that is consuming them.

If we will combine morality with compassion, if we will mean what we say and live what we believe, the world will crave the faith we have. They are watching what we do. We were not meant to be apathetic, lukewarm water, just going with the flow. We were meant to be living, reviving water that can satisfy the thirstiest souls! We were destined to be a radiant church, beaming hope to the nations. Now is the time to seize our beautiful fate. Each one of us has been given the power to change things.

The way we live is up to us.

Twenty-Two

Whirlwind Legacy

We walked beneath the crimson and orange brilliance of a twilit sky. The distant roar of the Jordan River flowed behind us, and a soothing breeze swept through the valley of the encompassing gorge. Scattered, lonely bushes swayed gently beneath the shadows cast by the magnificent crags that loomed above us. The heavens would soon explode in all its starry splendor, but now only a few faint stars began to wake above the rosy horizon.

The end was near. Soon Elijah would be swept up into the presence of God. This would be his final adventure.

Side-by-side, as master and apprentice, we journeyed on through the ravine talking together. Usually the fire of battle was in his eyes, for he had spent all his life tirelessly waging war against Israel's idolatry. But today only a warm glow emitted from his gaze, revealing such an inner tranquility that I felt my own heart engulfed in peacefulness.

For a brief moment our conversation ceased

as we walked on in contented silence. I could discern from his pensive countenance that he was preparing his next words with extra care. I absently studied the colorful evening sky as I waited for him to speak.

"Elisha . . ." he said quietly, summoning my attention once more. He paused after he spoke my name and smiled softly. The expression on his face and affectionate inflection he put into his voice in the way he said my name was that of a proud father to his son. These nuances brought great joy to my soul. Elijah was, after all, my role model, and his affirmation was more valuable to me than the world's most precious jewels.

"Tell me," he continued, "what can I do for you before I am taken from you?"

I thought carefully for a moment then, with a grin on my face, I answered, "Let me inherit a double portion of your spirit."

Elijah suddenly halted. His eyes grew and he gave out a surprised yet delighted laugh.

"You have asked a difficult thing," he exclaimed. His expression turned thoughtful as he squinted and stroked his beard to consider my request. After a short moment, as if having just discovered a revelation, new wisdom lit up his gaze as he said, "If you see me when I am taken from you, then you will have your request. But if not, then you won't."

He clutched the back of my arm, offered an intense, encouraging nod, then proceeded to walk on. I stood behind for a moment to reflect on his words. This would be the sign as to whether or not my request would be granted: all I had to do was fasten my eyes on my master, and if God would permit me perception to see Elijah's translation, I would take up his mantle. I yearned to do battle against the darkness with the power of light, just as my father in the faith had done. I wanted nothing more than to carry on his noble campaign. But I could not achieve victory in my own power. I needed supernatural prowess far beyond my own to walk in his footsteps. If a double portion of his spirit rested upon me, I knew nothing would be impossible for me.

While I was lost in my thoughts, Elijah strode a good ten paces ahead of me, so I hurried to catch up. When my stride finally matched his, we continued on in conversation. As he shared wisdom with me, I made sure to fix my eyes on his. Only God could grant me ability to see my master's departure, but I had to do my part by being ready and alert. It took no real effort to maintain attentiveness because his insights never failed to engross my eager mind.

But, all of a sudden, our conversation was interrupted when a faraway thunderclap reached our ears. We simultaneously spun around to find its source, and our eyes were dazzled by mountainous black clouds surfacing in the distance. Like a giant crouching behind a hiding place only to reveal himself to a terrified victim by quickly standing up to full stature, the monstrous clouds climbed above the horizon with phenomenal speed. The muffled thunderclap transformed into a shrieking peal as the clouds crept like reaching fingers across the sky, creating a canopy of impregnable shadow until it concealed the heavens. All at once, the shadow released a flood of thick raindrops, drenching us completely in a matter of moments. Lightning bolts sizzled furiously above us, and a towering tunnel of wind revolved no more than a mile away.

I looked on Elijah, his face lit by the flashing lightning, and I was surprised to discover him grinning from ear to ear as if he knew exactly what was happening. To my astonishment, he picked up where he left off in our conversation and continued walking. I let out a quiet laugh, remembering that supernatural occurrences were quite natural to Elijah, and continued walking with him. We didn't get far, though, because the distant cry of neighing horses filled the sky. Suddenly, steeds of fire pulling a chariot made of flames sped towards Elijah and me. The tunnel of swirling wind raced behind the blazing chariot, and it appeared we were going to get run over. They moved as rapidly as the blink of an eye. I had no time to react. The fiery horses galloped between us spraying flames into the sky, and the passing of the chariot covered us in a wave of heat. Immediately after they flew between us the ensuing whirlwind rushed on us, swept Elijah off his feet, and carried him into the air. The ferocious current missed me by only a hair's breadth, and I stood behind watching Elijah spinning into the sky.

"My father! My father!" I cried. "The chariots and horsemen of Israel!"

The soaring whirlwind twirled faster and faster, rapidly bearing Elijah upward. The fiery horses and chariot rounded off, then flew into the air and rushed fearlessly into the swirling current. The horses and chariot dashed up into the cloudy canopy, pulling the tunnel of wind behind them as if by an invisible cord. Elijah was carried up in the whirlwind to the clouds and beyond, disappearing from sight.

My beloved master was gone.

With my gaze still lifted, I tore my garment

in two and cried out in grief. I fell to my knees and held out my hands. I could feel drops of rain inter-mingled with fresh tears streaming down my face and falling off my jaw. The sizzle of lightning and the crashing of thunder filled my ears. The raging storm had managed to fight its way into my soul.

How could I go on without my father in the faith?

I stared through misty eyes at the black sky, hoping in vain that Elijah might come back down. But as I studied the stormy abyss above, I noticed something falling from the clouds. I wondered if my eyes were being cheated by some illusion my crazed mind had conjured, but when it was close enough for me to make out, I knew my mind was playing no trick. This was a sign sent from God Himself.

Elijah's mantle!

It must have escaped his shoulders as he rode the whirlwind. Now the mantle fell from Heaven to me. The symbol overwhelmed me. Elijah's spirit would remain with me in double portion. My request had been granted.

It fluttered down and crashed quietly in front of me. As soon as it touched the ground, the storm ceased. The pouring rain reduced to a light drizzle as if God poured out a bucket of water that was now emptied, leaking only a few drops. The lightning bolts vanished, and the cracks of thunder were silenced. The black blanket of clouds began to part, exposing patches of the dark blue evening sky. As the breeze sung softly into my ears, I rose to my feet and looked at the mantle.

All I had to do now was take it up.

I grabbed hold of it, draped it around my body, and lifted my gaze to observe the clearing sky. I thought back to the day I was first called by God: I was out plowing in the field with twelve oxen when Elijah approached me and cast this very mantle on my shoulders, symbolizing that I was destined to be a prophet. Now the mantle would permanently rest on my shoulders, and my destiny would be fulfilled.

I turned toward the Jordan River and fixed my eyes on the land of Israel which lay beyond it. With newfound purpose and resolve, I began the journey home. My soul was grieved because I knew I would not see Elijah in this world again, but I found unwavering hope as I called to mind the reality that he was present with the LORD even now, and he didn't even have to taste the bitter throes of death to get there! The presence of God that now engulfed him was also with me, and it was my duty to complete the work my master started.

I finally arrived at the brink of the river, and I knew it was time to put my anointing to the test. I stared at the running waters, anticipating my first miracle. This would be the final confirmation . . .

The parting of the Jordan River.

I folded my mantle like a rod, and the passion in my heart cried out, "Where is the LORD, the God of Elijah?" With all my might, I struck the waves with the mantle. Suddenly the waters on one side began to heap up as if crashing into an unseen embankment. It flowed upward like a thick, bubbling spring. On the other side the water fled towards the Dead Sea like an army retreating with all speed from its enemy. Joyful tears glazed my eyes. Shivers crawled down my spine. I walked through the Jordan on dry ground.

As I traveled the short distance to the other side, I realized the parting of the Jordan was not only my first miracle, but it was also the final miracle Elijah had performed. I was picking up where he left off.

Once both of my feet touched the other side, the invisible embankment crumbled and the water crashed onto the dry path once more. For a moment I watched the fallen heap hurry to catch up with the water that had been flowing away toward the Dead Sea, but when I turned around, I glimpsed from afar fifty prophetical students staring at me. Their jaws were dropped. One of them hit another student while gaping at me in disbelief, as if to say, *Did you see that? The Jordan divided for Elisha just like it did for Elijah! We are looking on the new prophet of Israel.*

I couldn't help but smile as I put the mantle back on my shoulders. Now I knew that I bore a double portion of Elijah's spirit . . .

Now I knew that his legacy would live on through me.

Twenty-Three

Determine Eternity

We only have one chance at life. Like a morning fog, life appears only for a little while before it evaporates and disappears forever. There is a day appointed for each man to die, and that day is approaching more quickly than we realize. God has given each of us only one life and one opportunity to live it to the fullest.

This is your chance to make it count.

What will be your legacy? How will people remember you after you die? No one will care about how big your bank account was, how many awards you won, or how many points you scored. Only the things you do for God will live on after you. The treasures of this world can be stolen, corrupted, and destroyed, but Heaven's luminous rewards never fade or grow dim. This life alone can only leave you empty and searching for more . . . even if you get to the very top. This was a fact King Solomon discovered: he had fame, power, a thousand wives and concubines, and he had amassed so much wealth that silver was as plentiful in Jerusalem as stones. He had it all . . . and he was miserable. "Meaningless! Meaningless!" he said. "Everything is meaningless." All this world can give is short-lived pleasure that leaves the heart hollow, longing, and devastated. Life is too brief to live for the things that won't last. It is a mere blink of an eye in comparison to eternity. But Heaven lasts forever. And ever. And ever. It *never* ends. It makes no sense to live for the unsatisfying "blink of an eye."

Put your stock in Heaven, because that is a market that will never crash.

Do not despair because life is short. Do not fear death. Jesus has defeated the grave, and your faith in Him is the key that opens the gates of eternity. He has gone to prepare a place just for you, that where He is there you may be also. Death is simply a door through which we all must pass. Soon you will gaze into the everlasting sunrise found in Jesus' eyes. Soon you will walk upon gleaming streets of gold. Your soul will leave the perishing tent it now inhabits, and it will finally make its home in a flawless body. Your eyes will awaken to an immortal dawn, and your feet will dig into the sand of crystal shores. Earth's greatest beauties are only cracked mirrors and poor reflections of the splendor Heaven contains. There your quests and adventures will truly begin. You can sing worship songs in harmony with David, walk on water beside Peter, and race chariots of fire against Elijah. The most captivating fantasies your imagination can evoke will finally be outdone. At last sorrow, evil, pain, and death will be swallowed up.

O death, where is thy sting? O grave, where is thy victory?

But eternal life doesn't just begin when you breathe your last. It starts *right now.* What you do here on earth determines what your forever will be. Your present decisions decide how bright your star will shine in the fields of eternity. Send as many treasures ahead to Heaven as you possibly can. The sky is the limit, and it's up to you to take advantage of the fleeting opportunity while your lungs still breathe the air of this world. Each moment you've been given is a treasure, and if you don't spend it for God now, it will vanish, forever void and tragically unused. Live each one to the fullest for God's Kingdom. Make it your goal to store more treasures in Heaven today than you ever have before, and your star will gain greater brilliance, a brilliance that the darkness can never touch.

This is your time. Mark the world for Jesus. The race is almost done, so run as fast as you can. Run. And win the prize.

Twenty-Four

A Prisoner's Destiny

Joseph sat in the dark confines of an Egyptian prison. He'd been sentenced for a crime he never committed. These were his reflections one winter's night:

It has been thirteen years.

Thirteen years since I arrived in this foreign land. It is difficult to believe I have been here for so very long. Then again, it feels as if I've been a prisoner forever, and at times I can't even recall what life was like as a free man. Ever since my brothers sold me into slavery, everything changed.

And I couldn't be more grateful that they did it . . .

You see, it all began when my father bestowed on me a coat of many colors. It was a symbol of favor that set me apart from my brothers. I was only seventeen years old, and I couldn't help but feel I was at the pinnacle of the world. Then, increasing the joy in that life of mine which was so untroubled, I dreamt twice that one day I would be elevated to a position of authority. In the first dream, I saw each of my brothers with a bundle of wheat, and their bundles fell reverently before mine. Soon after, I dreamed that the sun, moon, and eleven stars all bowed down to me.

I could not wait to tell my brothers!

They didn't exactly share in my enthusiasm.

It was then my fate appeared to take a turn for the worse. They were so furious with me that they threw me into an empty cistern before selling me to a caravan of Midianite traders. I was taken in chains to Egypt, and I started out as nothing more than a slave. But the LORD began to prosper the work of my hands, and I was given favor and responsibility. For a time, it seemed as though everything might unfold in a fortunate manner after all, but when I was falsely accused of committing a crime against my master, I was thrown into prison.

It was not bitterness or anger I felt, only brokenness. My hopes were shattered. Despair leaked into my heart. Any chance for my dreams seemed gone forever.

I am now thirty years old and am sitting in the very cell I was cast into all those years ago. Although I may be in the same place as far as location, I am in an entirely different place as a man. In fact, I no longer see this room as a prison cell at all . . . more as a room of education. Brokenness has taught me so much more than I ever imagined I could learn. God's Word lives within me and tests me every day. Slowly but without doubt, I am learning to pass the test by answering life's questions with faith. And although I cannot wait for my dreams to realize, I realize waiting is the only path to my dreams.

During my first year as a slave, I found myself faced with the difficult questions in life. And for the very first time, I wasn't certain how I was going to create the solutions. It was never before in my nature to doubt, but I began to discover that what I previously believed were the answers were actually the problems. I was perplexed, and the faster my head spun the more my faith careened out of control. It seemed as if I was being transformed into an entirely different person. I used to be so sure of myself, so sure of what I believed, so sure of my dreams. But the moment suffering entered my life, nothing was the same. Nothing was clear to me anymore.

I was in the darkness, alone with my thoughts.

I did not have many answers, but there was always one abiding foundation for my wandering feet: the LORD was the one truth I knew I could *forever believe. Even when I did not have the slightest idea where my journey was taking me, I knew in my heart that the working of His hands was beyond sight. I used to believe I had complete comprehension. I thought I had everything together.*

That is why I needed to be broken.

Little did I know, He was taking me apart so He could place me back together again. Now I understand that I could not see anything properly because I was blinded by my tears. But I also understand that my tears did not solely blind my vision, they also cleansed it. At last I can see the world with new eyes. Before my slavery, when I was still an adolescent in Canaan, I thought I could see perfectly. But my vision was clouded; I just didn't realize it. I did not know there was another way one could see. So when I was sold into bondage, I went from seeing only the happiness of life to being overwhelmed by the abject reality of suffering. I began searching frantically but was unable to find because I was blinded by my grief. Now, years later, God is wiping away my tears, and I can see more clearly than I ever have. It's as if I only saw in black and white, was suddenly blinded, and now my eyes are opening to the colors of the world. I see that my grief did not take away my vision, but clarified it.

I needed to unlearn so I could begin to truly

learn. I had to face doubt so I could grasp faith. I was taken apart so God could reshape me, and I was broken so I could see how frail I truly am.

I am a prisoner, and as far as circumstances, I couldn't be further away from my dreams. But I wouldn't choose any other course because now I cannot earn any credit when they come to pass. It will have to be a miracle, and only God can take the glory for a miracle.

I know a great deal about miracles.

My great-grandmother Sarah and my mother Rachel were both unable to have children. But God did a miracle for each of them. When Sarah was ninety years old she had Isaac. Isaac then had Jacob, my father, and Jacob married Rachel. Rachel was barren, but God miraculously gave her a child. That child was me. I should not even be here today. I'm a miracle. So no one can tell me God doesn't perform miracles.

I may be in this prison presently, but it won't always be so. This is only my training ground. There is no possible way I can be equipped for honor if I do not first learn humility. My strength cannot grow without first being broken down. The darkness has taught me to discover the light, and the night is the only door through which the dawn can enter.

I could not be more pleased with the course

God has placed me on because I know it leads to my destiny. I have no idea how my dreams will come to fruition, but I know they are on their way. God always has perfect timing . . .

Joseph's thoughts were suddenly interrupted when a man flung open the prison door.

"Joseph," he said, "the pharaoh calls you up."

Twenty-Five

Race to the Future

Our yesterdays are spent waiting for tomorrow, but today is the tomorrow we've been waiting for. The sky is the limit for your God-given potential, but you'll never apprehend the stars while you're stuck in yesterday's prison. The chains of the past will be broken by the power your future contains.

Your destiny starts now. Today is a memory to be made. Today's actions can be Heaven's treasures rather than tomorrow's regrets.

God has put eternity into your hands, fashion it into a masterpiece that will awaken the dreams in others. Your vision can open eyes that have lost sight, and your steps of faith can leave footprints for them to follow. Don't wait to relinquish the weight of the past; the race to the future is run only on the course of today.

Life is in this very moment. Today is the initiation of tomorrow's dreams. Begin your pursuit of the plans the Lord has fashioned for you.

Your faith can gain on the Promised Land

and your courage can vanquish the giants. Desire can take the mountains and obedience can raze the walls. Your battles will be a channel for gifts of comfort to souls writhing in defeat. Your losses will bring them hope. The scars your adventures have purchased can heal their deepest wounds, and your wholehearted charity can piece together their broken hearts.

Reaffirm the inspiration of creative, child-like faith, and shine your good works into the darkness until your star adorns the fields of Heaven. Love Jesus more than your strongest passions and worship Him as if you never had another chance. When you fall, get back up, because your mistakes are the foundations of redemption. Forgive the darkest atrocities others have committed and accept God's forgiveness for your own. Surprise a world that is so used to bad news with the good news of salvation, and do not be ashamed of the Gospel you live for. Rejoice when you suffer shame for His Name, because in every reviling shout of persecution there is a hidden whisper of God's love.

Capture the Kingdom of Heaven with your prayers and kindle anthems of hope like living fire in your soul. Rejoice in the day that the Lord has made for you and redeem the invaluable time that you've been given. Stand strong on every promise and cherish every moment. Chase after the heart of God, and reach for your dreams.

The future begins now.